Coming Home

Darla Hagan

Coming Home

Darla Hagan

Copyright: Darla Hagan

Published: 2 January 2015

Publisher: Darla Hagan

The rights of Darla Hagan to be identified as author of this work has been asserted by her in accordance with section 77 and 78 of the Copyright Designs and Patents Acts 1988. All rights reserved. No part of this publication may be reproduced, stored in retrieval system, copied in any form or by any means, electronic, mechanical, photocopying, recording or otherwise transmitted without written permission from the publisher. You must not circulate this book in any form.

Coming Home

Darla Hagan

This book is a work of fiction. The characters, incidents, and dialogue are drawn from the author's imagination and are not to be construed as real. Any resemblance to actual events or persons, living or dead, is entirely coincidental.

Coming Home

DEDICATED

To My Family

Acknowledgments

First and foremost I have to thank my family and friends for all the encourgement they gave me during the writing of this book. A special thanks to both my sisters, Linda and Diana for all the editing and re-reads, and changes, and re-reads, and for putting up with me all hours of the night, and doing it all with a smile. I have the best group of people on my side and I can't wait to finish the next book in the series.

Coming Home

Chapter 1

Abigail Laurence stood in the cold damp air with a blanket around her shoulders watching the home she grew up in slowly crumbling into a fiery pile of ash. She didn't cry or show any kind of emotion. She just watched and thought back on all the times she would run down those stairs when her Mother called her for breakfast, or to do chores. She thought of the curtains her Mother had made in the kitchen, of that raggedy chair that Dad would sit in and read the morning paper and watch TV in the evening. Mom hated that chair. Old Pink she called it. The room she shared with her identical twin sister Julie and all the secrets they would tell late at night. The giggles and tears, the heartbreaks and fears, all coming to mind as it was all disappearing in slow motion before her eyes. "You okay Miss?" I was drawn from my thoughts. "What? Oh, yes, I'm fine." I said with a fake smile. Of course I'm not fine, you idiot, my house is burning to the ground. All my childhood memories, pictures, the growth notches marked in the hallway, and Daddy's chair. That old piano that Julie and I both hated but had to take lessons because Mom wanted us to be ladies and ladies played the piano. Daddy just wanted us to be us.

It has been very hard to come back here after the accident that took both my parents. When Julie arrived she had her hair cut in a short bob and it was black with burgundy highlights. It's rather strange to see your own reflection in someone else's face especially looking so different. We are in our forties, tall, and I wear my blonde hair long and straight. I can pull it up when it's hot and wear a hat without having to worry about getting hat hair. I knew Julie would look different but was not prepared for this. I try to exercise and run when I can. I am proud of my body. I feel good about the way I look at my age. It gets harder every year to keep it that way. Julie looks like she has spent a lot of time in a lounge chair soaking up sun and eating bon bons.

After the shock of seeing her we went to work on what to do. We decided I would buy her half of the house and divide everything else as was in the will. She chose some things from the house that she wanted and I kept the rest. She has been missing from my life

Coming Home

for quite some time now, and she only called Mom and Dad by phone on Birthdays and Christmas. She always had some excuse to not come but would always call. We've never met her husband but do know that they travel a lot. She never had children that we know of and I had no way to reach her when Mom and Daddy passed but an old cell number. I took my chances and left a voice mail. It worked and she showed but we have grown so far apart, it wasn't even good to see her. She's almost a stranger to me. We were so close when we were young. She cried to all our friends and said she should never have left. I thought it all strange that she would care that much given the circumstances but I guess we all grieve in our own way. After the graveside service, she didn't say anything to anyone, just got in a limo and rode away, again. It was like she was never there.

I had a thriving business and living in Houston at the time and was really exploring the idea of moving back to Wimberley to get out of the hectic traffic and crazy pace. Back to the small town tranquility and the beautiful Texas Hill Country people. After my parents died, I made the decision to do just that. I sold my business and moved back here to Wimberley to open a Boutique. I have only been here for three months and getting the store ready has taken most of my time. I haven't even changed anything in the house and most of my things are still in storage. I guess now that is a good thing.

Jamie, my insurance agent broke my thoughts

hugging me and saying "Oh honey, I'm so sorry. Don't you worry about a thing. You are heavily insured and I will take care of everything." "Thank you Jamie. I am just numb right now. I don't feel anything." "That is a normal reaction when something like this happens. Do you have a place to stay?" "Yes, I can stay in the cabin." The Cabin. Daddy built it when Julie and I were young, by the river on the back of the property, or the front depending on whether you call the riverside the front or the road side the front! It has two bedrooms and two bathrooms. Daddy said "If there are two women in a house there has to be two bathrooms!" I'm sure I will have to air it out again from all the smoke, but it should be fine for just me. With all my things still in storage, I will easily be able to furnish a new house.." "Well, okay, if you need anything, you just let me know." With a kiss on the cheek she was gone.

I have known Jamie since grade school. She is a feisty little red head with a huge heart and a contagious laugh. We lost touch after high school but in a small town old friends remain friends no matter the distance or time between them. It was good to feel that in her hug.

A large part of the town had been there to watch the happenings but most were dispersed and only one fire truck remained. One of the firemen came over to tell me most of the problem was under control but they would remain for several hours just to watch for hot spots that might flare up. I thanked him and told him I would be staying in the cabin at the bottom of the hill.

Coming Home

He asked if the water supply was city or well and I told him well. He said "You'll be fine then. Tomorrow there will probably be some folks coming out to investigate the origin of the fire. Please don't cross the taped area until they have completed their investigation." "I won't sir. Thank you and all your men for what you did tonight." "We're just doing our job ma'am. You take care now." He said with a smile and a tip of his hat.

Mom and Dad had refurbished the cabin when Tessa, my daughter, started college. She would bring her friends just like Julie and I used too. Tessa had mentioned it was an excellent place to bring her friends but had been so busy this past year, she never got a chance to come. After she told me this I decided to air it out and freshen it up just in case she could find the time. I had a cleaning service come in and clean from top to bottom so at least I am one step ahead of the game.

I knew there would be items I would need so I decided I had better get to the store. I was still in my running clothes but that would have to do. Since the wind was blowing the smoke in the opposite direction of the cabin I went in and opened all the windows and turned on the giant attic fan to clear out any lingering smoke smell. I took a quick inventory of what I would need for the night, turned on the water, hot water heater and refrigerator. I had my list in hand and before I headed to the store I decided to leave the windows open and hope the wind did not change direction. My basket was so full I could barely push it, and that's just the basics. I would buy wine and remember I didn't have anything to drink it out of, so I had to buy glasses, soap, shampoo, conditioner, toothpaste, tooth brush. Good grief I'm never gonna get all this in that cabin! I don't even have underwear or pajamas or clothes! Three hundred dollars and a car full later, I am on my way. I feel like a homeless person. Oh wait, I am a homeless person! The realization brought tears to my eyes and all the pent up quiet just broke loose. I had to pull over and stop. I was back sitting around the dinner table talking about school and work. I could smell Mom's pot roast and homemade biscuits. She always made enough gravy to cover everything. If that wasn't enough, there was some wonderful dessert to finish it off. I didn't know how much I loved and missed those days till now.

Julie and I decided to go to college close to home, and chose Texas State in San Marcos. At the time they called it Southwest Texas State but changed the name later. I am still not quite sure why. We shared a dorm room, studied together, went out together and spent a lot of weekends at the cabin. She was always easy going and come what may, and sometimes I had to rein her in a little. In our third year of college, I met Jimmy. He immediately captured my heart with his charm and good looks. We started dating and became very close. Julie could not stand him and made no attempt to hide it. She would tell me he wasn't good for me but I fell head over heels and in June I found out I was pregnant. Jimmy was furious and wanted me to

Coming Home

have an abortion but I would have nothing to do with it, so we got married. We got an apartment off campus which left Julie completely out of the picture. I would try to do things with her when I wasn't working or studying but she would always be busy. She even quit coming home on weekends. She would tolerate Jimmy when she had to, like Christmas and family gatherings but never went out of her way to be nice. When we graduated Julie went to California. She kept in touch but barely. She didn't even let us know where in California she was. All we had was the cell phone number she left with us. I dried my face, took a few deep breaths, and started for home.

    I had not realized just how tired I was until I got on that lonely curvy road home. I turned the radio up really loud and turned the air conditioner on freeze your ears mode to stay awake. I arrived at the cabin safe and sound and began to unload everything. It smelled much better, so I shut the windows and turned off the fan. I bought some wax burners to give the place a pleasant floral odor. I was going to get smelly candles but given what just happened quickly eighty- sixed that idea! I put all the cold stuff away, filled the bathroom with the necessary items, grabbed a blanket, and went out on the porch to lie in the hammock for a while. I could hear the soothing sound of the river running over rocks and fallen trees. I could smell the lingering effects of the smoke. My ears finally thawed and the warmth of the evening was allowing every muscle in my body to relax. I slipped into a deep peaceful sleep.

Darla Hagan

I love fall in Texas. It can be forty one day and ninety the next but the nights are usually very pleasant. Because of this I was awakened by the sun, still in the same position I was in when I laid down. The wind had changed and the strong odor of smoke and burned wood filled my nose and brought me back to reality. I am glad I shut all the windows before I went out.

I rolled myself out of the hammock and headed to the shower. I turned on the water, got undressed and let the water just run over me. I soaped and shampooed and soaped and shampooed again. I wanted all that smoke smell off me. When I finally felt I was as clean as I could get and running out of hot water, I gave up. I actually smelled pretty good, and made my way to the kitchen to make some coffee. Now, if I can just find the sack the coffee is in!

Standing by the kitchen window looking out at the rubble, I was taking in the whole scene. The house was originally built on pier and beam. About a year ago a sun room was added using a concrete slab. Daddy said it just made sense but I always thought it took away from the charm of the house. What this means is if I decide to rebuild, all that will have to be broken up and removed. It will have to be completely scraped away and start from scratch. It's too soon for me to even wrap my head around all of it. I am looking at the ashes that used to have laughter, tears, break ups, and family times pouring out of it. Those times seem even more precious now. One of the fireman asked me last night not to cross the tape until the investigators

Coming Home

have been out to inspect and make their decision of the origin of the fire. As much as I would love to get in there and look around, I will abide by their rules and stay away.

Darla Hagan

Chapter 2

The huge rock fireplace is still standing but charred with smoke and ash. The sun room seemed to have taken the least of the damage but I am sure the water took its toll on the contents. I did have pictures and such packed in plastic containers in that room and hopefully some of them survived. There's Mom and Dad's wedding photos, Julie's and my graduation, birthdays, and Christmas. Oh we had such wonderful times at Christmas. Mom would cook for days, and Daddy would decorate the outside of the house with a zillion lights. On Christmas Eve we got to open one present but the rest had to wait until Christmas Day. Such wonderful childhood memories. I come back to the real world and have a feeling I'm gonna be in this cabin for a while. This was our party house. I think Daddy built it just for Julie and me. He felt if the parties were here he could always know where his girls were. He overlooked a lot of craziness during that time, and deep in his heart I think he enjoyed every minute of it.

An official looking truck pulls up and two men with clip boards get out. One is of average height, balding, and looks like he enjoys eating a lot of fried foods. The other is tall, nice build, dark hair showing beneath a cowboy hat, and a very nicely trimmed beard and mustache. Maybe I should introduce myself and see if there are any questions I can answer. I quickly run to the bathroom, finish drying my hair, throw on a little mascara, grab a T-shirt, some jeans, and tennis shoes. Another quick glance in the mirror and out the back door I go.

They both look up when they hear the screen door squeak. I walk up the hill, give a little wave, and say "Hi." They both tip their hats and respond with "Good Morning." The taller one puts his pen on his clipboard and walks toward me. He removes his sunglasses and I am staring at the darkest blue eyes I've ever seen. He extends his hand and asks "Are you Ms. Laurence?" "Yes, I'm Abby Laurence." "I'm Cade Tate. I am a laboratory analyst and this is George Rancher the fire scene investigator." Mr. Rancher nodded his head and continued his probing. I ask "Is there anything you need to know or that I may be able to help you with?"

"I would like to speak to you after we take a few samples and look around. Are you planning on leaving soon?" "No, I have no plans other than putting away things in my new home" I pointed to the cabin "and calling the necessary people to start the cleanup process." "Well don't send out the bulldozers just yet. We should be finished in an hour or so and we will come and talk with you then." "Okay, I will see you in a little while." He then smiled, turned to walk back to the mess that was left of my house.

I just stood there for a few seconds trying to catch my breath. I watched him walk away and noted his muscular arms pushing against the material of his shirt. He also had on nicely fitting khaki slacks that hugged equally muscular legs and a tight little butt. He finished all this off with a nice pair of Ostrich cowboy boots that showed just right from under the slacks. I finally closed my mouth and turned to walk back to the cabin. I tripped on a stump and went stumbling down the hill till I hit the cabin. I turned around, smiled, and rolled myself around the corner of the cabin till I was out of view. Damn me and my clumsy self. I don't know why it happens whenever I'm trying to be so cool. My brain cells go dead and all the things that are supposed to work just go to mush!

Oh my gosh, I need to straighten up this place. I haven't put away the stuff from last night and I need to make up my bed, and clean up the bathroom. I turned on the scented wax smelly things and got busy. As I was finishing up the coffee pot I could see them concentrating on one area and wondered if they had found the reason for the fire. They are shaking their heads and writing on their little clipboards. They dust off their hands and put the things away in the truck. They are now headed my way and Cade has a different type of clipboard in his hand. I quickly move away from the window and try to make myself look busy. I hear the footsteps on the porch and the knock on the door. I walk in from the other room looking all surprised. "Oh hi, please come in. May I get you something to drink?" "No ma'am but thank you." "Have a seat. I'm sorry about the smell. I tried to air it out all last night but it seems to want to linger." "Believe me ma'am this smell is all too familiar. I have to analyze some things back at the lab and file a report but our preliminary findings are faulty wiring in the attic. Because the house was temporarily empty it was probably rodents chewing on the wires. The main part seems to have started in the living area and spread from room to room. When a fire starts in the upper portion of the house there is usually less damage to the lower floors. In your case, with the age of the house and the rural area, it takes a little longer to get to the fire and therefore you have a little more damage to those floors. We will most likely be ruling the fire accidental and you should be able to start working on clearing and rebuilding in a couple of weeks." "Wow, you found out all of that in that short time?" "We've seen many of these cases and pretty much know what to look for. I will have everything typed up and bring it out for you to read and sign. After that the rest is up to you and your insurance company." "Thank you again gentlemen for your courteous and prompt help." They stood to leave and Cade signed off on what he had just discussed with me and that's when I noticed he was left handed, and that left hand had a ring on it. "I'll be by with the paperwork as soon as I can. It was nice meeting you Ms. Laurence." "You too gentlemen and thank you both again."

Oh my, I ran to the kitchen window just to watch him walk away. Damn he sure wears his clothes well. "Stop it." I said to myself. You're practically engaged. I don't think Luke would be very happy with the thoughts running through my mind right now. Mr. Tate is clearly married. I doubt his wife would like the way I am ogling her husband.

As it turns out Julie was right, Jimmy was not a good husband or father. We had one daughter, Tessa. She was the most perfect little baby girl. She had the greenest eyes you've ever seen, and her Dad's olive complexion set off with my blonde hair. She grew to despise him. He became verbally abusive and distant, and after years of being home very little, we gave it up. I was devastated after the separation. I tried to stay strong for Tessa but depression overcame me and I ended up living with Mom and Dad for a while until I finally pulled myself out of that dark hole and got on with my life. Tessa was not in school yet so she was not upset at all about staying with Gran and Pop.

Jimmy paid child support and now pays for

Coming Home

Tessa's college but that comes in the form of a check through the court. I've had no communication with him for many years. He gave me the house and I opened my own business after a short while. Tessa spent her school years in Houston and decided to go to her Mom's alma mater for college which was another reason for coming back to Wimberley.

I met Luke through a mutual friend and in time we became close even though our relationship is a long distance one. Always has been. He lives in Temple and I lived in Houston. Now I'm in Wimberley and he still lives in Temple. I love him and love being with him but he can't leave his job and I need to be here. Especially now. I really should call him to let him know about the house but I'm not ready to answer all his questions just yet. I will wait until this evening after he gets home from work. I do, however, need to talk with Tessa. She loved this house as much as I did. She would spend a lot of summers here with Gran and Pop. She is in her last year unless she decides to go for her Masters. She is majoring in business, following in her Mom's footsteps at Texas State, so she's not that far from home and we see each other whenever we can.

Tessa was, of course, very distraught to hear the news but took it better than I thought she would. She asked if she should come home this weekend and I said that was up to her but I would be so busy with the shop we would not get to visit much. She opted to wait and I am glad. She said "Are you sure you're okay Mom?" I said "I'm fine Sweetie. I'll see you when things settle down." "I love you." "I love you too Baby. Bye bye." I then called Luke and told him the news. "What? Are you Okay?" "Other than the fact that my house is gone I'm fine!" "I can be there in three hours." "No Luke just wait until Friday. There is nothing you can do. I have to sort out some things and I don't feel that I would be giving you any attention." "I love you my sweet, you are strong and we can get through this together." "I love you too, Luke. Goodnight."

When I hung up I realized just how much the day had taken its toll on me, I ran a warm bath in the old claw footed tub that's perfect for a leisurely soak. I got a glass of wine and turned on some music. The temperature was a little warmer than I expected and I had to slowly lower the sensitive areas in. Once settled it felt wonderful. I took a good long drink of the wine and let my troubles drift away to complete relaxation. I was letting my arms just float and zoning out when the damn phone broke into my quiet peaceful place. Who the hell would be calling now? I let the machine pick up as I was not giving up my tranquility for a stinking phone call. I heard a man's voice and listened as Cade Tate tells me "Uh, Hi Ms. Laurence, this is Cade Tate, I just wanted to let you know I finished the report and will come by tomorrow to have you sign the final papers. Then you should be able to proceed with your insurance. If it is okay I will come by around noon. If there is a problem please call the office and let me know. It was a pleasure meeting you and have a good evening." Wow, that was really quick I thought to myself.

Coming Home

I have rented a building in the market district or old downtown area and am opening a retail boutique. The Grand Opening is this week. Since it is fall I am only going to be open Thursday thru Sunday. Tomorrow is Wednesday and I will have to wait for Cade to come by with the paperwork before I can go see Jamie. She will be expecting me so it should be a fairly easy process. I drag myself from the tub, dry off and pretty much fall into the bed in a wine stupor and drift off to dreamland.

I actually slept till ten and it felt so good. I really need to get to the store after I finish with Cade and Jamie. There are a few last minute things that need to be done. I was cleaning up my brunch dishes when I heard Cade's truck in the driveway. I dried off my hands and ran to the bathroom for a quick glance in the mirror then heard the knock on the door. I straightened out my shirt and said "it's open come on in." "Hi Abby, how are you?" "Just fine Cade. Do you have the paperwork for me? I really need to get to the insurance company so I can go to the store and prepare for tomorrow." "Yes ma'am. I have it right here. Just sign right here and I will be on my way." "I don't mean to be rude. I just have a million things to do and not enough time." "I understand, here's your copy to give to the insurance agent and you should be good to go." "Thank you Cade, I am going to follow you out." "Have a good day ma'am." "You too, if you need something special for your wife you should come by the shop. I have lots of really cute things." "Maybe another time, thanks."

Jamie was ready when I arrived and said "Hi Abby, I've got everything ready for you. I just need the paperwork from the fire agency." "Got it right here." "I am so sorry Abby. This is just awful. The company should have a check out to you within two weeks. If you haven't heard from them by then, let me know." "I will, thanks Jamie. You've been wonderful." "I know that house had a lot of memories for you and me for that matter. We spent a lot of fun evenings out there." "Yeah, they were great." "Are you gonna rebuild?" "I'm not sure yet. It's something I will have to think about for a while and right now I'm so into the boutique, I just don't have the time. Thank goodness for the cabin." "Oh I forgot about the cabin. We had so much fun in that place." She said with a giggle. We spent more than a few sleep overs and afternoon swimming parties together. "Thanks Jamie, I've gotta run. I still have to do some finishing touches on the place before the big opening tomorrow. Come by and take a look around." "I'll be there, if you need anything Abby, don't hesitate to ask." "I won't, thanks again."

Coming Home

Chapter 3

I decided to go by the storage unit. I had only been in town for three months and most of that time was spent getting the store ready. I hadn't really moved anything of my own in the house other than clothes and shoes. When I sold the house in Houston, I just had everything packed and moved to the storage unit. There just hadn't been time to unpack anything. I had been going through pictures and such at night and packing them in plastic containers. Most of which I was storing in the sun room. Maybe, just maybe some things survived. I left the storage units without even getting out of the car. That would just have to wait.

Darla Hagan

I drove home noticing the beauty of the colors the cypress trees were showing. I had forgotten how beautiful they were this time of year. I crossed the small low water crossing and pulled into the lane past what was left of the house and drove on down to the cabin. I went inside, changed into old jeans, a t-shirt, and old tennis shoes. It was time to see what was salvageable. Glass crunched under my shoes as I walked through what used to be the kitchen. The old kitchen table where we had such good talks and laughs, even an occasional food fight, was nothing but charred pieces with melted metal pieces here and there. Mom's aluminum stool she used when ironing was a melted pool of silver with a hint of burnt yellow plastic from the cushion cover. I moved to the living room and there stood the metal springs and frame from Daddy's chair. My heart cracked and I couldn't stop the tears. I squatted down and put my head in my hands and let them flow. I felt a strong hand on my shoulder and thought for a moment Daddy was there telling me "It's gonna be fine girl." Then I realized there was a warm body attached to that arm and looked up suddenly to find Cade Tate beside me. It scared me so that I lost my balance and fell on my butt. "I'm sorry. I didn't mean to frighten you. I thought you heard me drive up." "Well I didn't and you scared the life out of me. What are you doing here?" "I was driving by and saw you, thought you might need someone to talk to. It is another part of my job, victim assistance." "Oh, I see."

He helped me up and I walked in the ashes and charred wood that used to be home and said "I really

Coming Home

didn't think it would be this hard. I mean I haven't lived here for twenty five years but there are so many memories." He took me by the shoulders and said "That's what you have to hang on to, is the memories. Go through pictures or anything you have to remind you." I looked at him with a surprised look and said "Pictures!" I moved quickly passed him to the sun room and found most of the plastic boxes melted with few remains. In the far corner were several that seemed somewhat intact. I ran to them and brushed away the water and ash sludge. "They're okay!" I laughed and looked up at him. "They're okay. Here's Mom and Dad's wedding pictures, and my graduation, and me and Julie playing on that swing out by the water. Oh these are wonderful. Would you help me move these to my porch?" He smiled real big and said "I'd be happy to help." He picked up one of the sludge covered boxes and started walking toward the cabin. I was watching him as he walked away and thought how nice it was of him to be here. We salvaged six boxes in all, some of which were in better shape than others but it was the only thing left of my childhood home. "Thank you for your help. I'm okay now, and I need to call someone to come out and clear all this away. I can't bear to look at it this way." "I'd be happy to stay and help." I was staring at the river and turned to look at him. "Oh no, you've done enough. I'll be fine. Thank you again." "You're very welcome, and you have my card if you decide you need to talk or have any more questions." "Yes, I do, and I will." "Well goodbye Abby Laurence. You take care." With a tip of his hat, he was gone.

Darla Hagan

I finally got to the store to add the finishing touches for tomorrow's sale. Anything to take my mind off the fire and the mess it left. I know everyone in town, at least all the locals will be by the store with condolences and gossip. Just one more thing you have in a small town. When I arrived I noticed Harriet's car and wondered why she was there. When I unlocked the back door and went inside, she was standing on a small step ladder hanging a sale sign. "What are you doing here?" "Well you've pretty much had your hands full so I figured I'd get this done so you wouldn't have to worry about it." She said as she was coming down the ladder. She walked toward me and with a big hug asks, "How are you Honey?" Harriet was a beautiful plump angel that could sell you the shirt off your back. Everyone loved her and I am so blessed to have her in my life. "I'm really doing pretty well. I've got all my ducks in their rows and am living in the cabin. I may have to use some of my inventory to dress myself but other than that, things are okay." "Have you talked to Luke?" "Yes, he'll be here Friday as usual. I think by then I'm really gonna need his shoulder." "Good, I want you to take off this weekend. My niece is coming in tomorrow and we can handle anything that might come up." "Oh Harriet, I can't do that. It's my Grand Opening and I want to be here."

I have known Harriet since I was born basically and she has taken it upon herself to be my keeper since my parents died. I know not to argue with her and trust her with my life. "Harriet, what would I do without you?" "You wouldn't! What do you think about this?"

Coming Home

She holds up a cute little dress. "It's your size and it will look good on you." "Yeah, since you've pretty much done everything I'm gonna go through and grab a few things. It feels really weird shopping in my own store." We finished up and I loaded my car with my things. I noted for inventory, and tax purposes all my purchases. "Goodnight Harriet. I'll see you in the morning. Are you picking up the pastries and wine or am I?" "I'll get it, you just get some rest." "I tell you what I'll pick up the pastries, they are on my way." "Okay hon, see you later."

I wasn't really interested in food but made myself a ham sandwich and settled in front of the TV for a while. The red wine I chose to go with it was taking off the edge and relaxing some of the tension in my muscles. The phone rang and I answered "Hi how's my love tonight?" "Well I was going to ask you the same thing but it sounds like you're doing pretty well." "I am sitting here with my feet up sipping on a very large glass of red wine. It doesn't get much better than that." "You do sound relaxed." "I am. I got the paperwork from the insurance company, and thanks to my wonderful assistant I am ready for my Grand Opening tomorrow." "I haven't had as good a day as you. I got served with papers today." "Oh Crap, what does she want this time?" "She's decided she wants more money for Jeffery's tuition." "I thought that was all settled." "Apparently she wants more." I have to go to court Friday morning and don't know when I'll be able to get away." "Its fine, you have to do what you have to do. I won't be home till late anyway." "I love you and I will see you soon." "Good luck and Goodnight."

Luke's divorce has been anything but amicable. He volunteered to pay half of the college tuition for each of their two sons but she's never happy. She did finally sign the divorce papers but continues to bring things like this back into play. It's really stressful for Luke and I feel I need to be there to support him. He takes such good care of me, and was there through my losing Mom and Dad. I love him dearly but sometimes there's just something missing from the relationship. Sometimes I feel like I want more but want Luke too. I could never hurt him. Our relationship is very comfortable for lack of a better word. Sleep came easy after a warm shower to wash away the fuzz and dust from the store.

In the morning I made a cup of coffee and watched the news. I don't know why I do this. It is always, death, politics, and celebrities. I turned it off, got dressed and made my way to the store. In the fall, business on Thursday and Friday is usually slow but with the Grand Opening I feel it will be pretty steady. Hopefully it will take my mind off my other problems and Luke will understand. "Hi Harriet, I should have known you'd be here before me." "Lots to do today girlie. I made the coffee, do you need help with the pastries?" "If you would just hold the door for me I think I can handle it." I gave her a big hug and said "I love you." "I know" she said with a smile. "Now let's get ready to rock this town."

Coming Home

Just as I predicted, the crowd was great. Of course a lot of the locals came out to talk about the fire. The sales were awesome and we are going to be here most of the night restocking. After a couple of hours I told Harriet "You go on home, you've been at this for days, and I know you are tired." "No I'm fine, and we need to put this place back together." "I can do it. It won't take that long. Here's a bottle of wine, go home, put your feet up and pop the cork." "I can't do that to you." "You can and you will. Now get out of here!" I said with a smile. "Well okay but don't forget those bracelets are on the top shelf, and the boots are arranged by size and." I shoved her out the back door and said "Goodnight Harriet." "Oh okay, Goodnight, you stubborn child." I laughed as she got in her car and drove away.

I waved and shut the door. I grabbed an open bottle of wine and poured myself a glass to drink while I straightened and restocked. I turned the music up and got down to business. I was finished by nine, turned everything off, rechecked the locks and made my way to the cabin. Just as I walked in the door the phone was ringing. It was Luke and I answered with a very tired "Hi baby." "Long day huh? You sound tuckered out! How did it go today?" "It was great but yes I am pooped. I don't even think I'm going to eat. I'm just going to shower and hit the sheets." "I won't keep you then. I love you and I'll see you tomorrow night." "I love you too. Goodnight." I did grab a piece of cheese and a couple of crackers as I was coming out of my clothes on the way to the bathroom. The shower was quick and then off to bed for me. I don't even remember my head hitting the pillow!

Friday was another busy day at the store and Harriet and I both knew Saturday was gonna be a killer, so when her niece arrived, she came straight to the store. She wanted to get adjusted before tomorrow. Her name is Cheryl and she's an absolute dream. When something goes out the door she's looking for something to put in it's place. "I want to adopt you Cheryl. Are you available?" We all laugh and get back to customers. There will definitely be something extra in her paycheck. Due to Cheryl's efforts we were pretty much ready for Saturday at the day's end. When I arrived home I saw Luke's car in the drive. It was such a welcome sight. He was in the hammock and said "There's my little lady. Did you have another busy day?" "Oh Luke", I said as I crawled in beside him. "I'm, exhausted." "I thought you might be so I bought something to eat." "You are the best, I'm starving." He pushed me out of the hammock and said "Let's eat. I've got the table set, the wine is poured, and the food is warming in the oven."

I blew out the candles and said "I am just a little freaked these days about fire." He takes my hand from across the table and says "Abby, I am so sorry about the house." That's when the dam broke again. He jumped up and took me over to the couch and just held me as I cried about pictures, furniture, and memories. I just shook with sobs. He held me and just kept saying "It's gonna be fine baby", and rocking me. I cried till I thought I had nothing left. He pulled me back and looked me in the eye and said "I will take care of you, just hold on to me." That started the whole thing over again. He ran me a warm bath with soft music and a glass of wine. He helped me undress and pulled up a stool to sit on and talk. The bath, the wine, and the food were just what I needed. "Luke this is so sweet. I love you so much." He dried me off, led me to the bedroom and tucked me in. A little while later he quietly crawled in. His arms surrounded me and I drifted off to a slumber without dreams.

I woke to the smell of coffee and turned over to find myself alone in the bed. I drug myself out and put on my robe. I saw him standing over the kitchen sink, coffee cup in hand staring out the window. I wrapped my arms around his waist and lay my head against his back. "Sorry I conked out on you last night." He turned around, held me and gave me a quick kiss. "It's quite alright Ms. Laurence. I was tired myself. I have been staring out this window and it sure looks strange without the house there." "I know, and as soon as I get this Grand Opening done I will start making arrangements to clear the debris and go from there. Right now I'm content right here." "I love you Abby and I am so sorry this happened." "I know Luke. I got a cup of coffee and headed to the bathroom to get ready for the day. I felt bad that I had not said I love you too but it just didn't feel right for some reason. I do love him and it has always been my choice to keep it long distance. I could have relocated in Temple but chose not to. I am a very outgoing person and love to do just about anything. Luke is more a stay at home and do nothing guy. He's so jealous that I am comfortable when we are with friends. He thinks I should be right by his side every minute. It's really hard to be me, the real me when he is around. He depends on me to be his rock and I can't deny him that. I treasure our time together but long for letting loose now and then.

He comes in behind me with a toasted English muffin covered in peanut butter and bananas, kisses me on the cheek and says "You better get a move on." "What are you gonna do today?" "I might fish a little, watch a game, and then I'm gonna fix you dinner." "How did I get so lucky to have you? I grab my muffin, my purse, give him a quick kiss and say as I'm walking out the door "I'll see you around six." "Why six? Don't you close at five?" "Yes but we have to straighten everything, restock, and be prepared for Sunday." There's that attitude of needing to know where I am every minute. "Love you." I said as I ran out the door.

Harriet and Cheryl were just pulling up as I arrived. I had stopped to pick up more treats for the day and another case of wine. "Hi ladies, are you ready for today?" "As ready as we'll ever be. Do you need some help?" "Please, Harriet, would you unlock the door and Cheryl, there are some pastries on the other side of the car. I'll grab the wine." The day was outrageous. We ran out of pastries, wine and are clearly going to have to get serious about our inventory before next week. A lot of out of state people were in

Coming Home

town and they believe you can't visit Texas without coming home with some boots and a cowboy hat. Anything western and blingy was sailing out the doors. I only sell the best brands. I try to deal with the local artist and jewelry makers, which in turn helps the economy of the town two fold. The key to good business is friendly and knowledgeable staff. I can really turn on the charm when I want to. You give me a man looking for a gift for his wife and I will send him home lighter in the pocketbook and with one very happy wife.

Just as promised Luke was working on supper when I arrived. It was ten of six so that made him happy. He had the grill going and was just waiting to throw the steaks on. "How about a glass of wine in the swing before supper?" "Oh Luke, that sounds like heaven." He helped me off with my boots and it felt good to have my feet free. I wiggled my toes and he poured the wine. We sat swinging and listening to the sounds of the evening. It was getting a little cool once the sun was completely down so Luke grilled the steaks and I set the table. He had baked potatoes with all the trimmings and also grilled asparagus. It was wonderful and felt so comfortable and right. We cleaned the dishes, took a shower and crawled in the hammock under a blanket. The night sky was clear with a quarter moon and stars everywhere. The crickets were chirping and somewhere in the distance was the hoot hoot from an owl. I kissed Luke and said "Let's go to bed." We didn't make love just cuddled and slept. At least Luke did. I was in his arms feeling completely alone.

Darla Hagan

Sunday is going to be another killer day and then we will have a few days to regroup. Luke will be headed back to Temple before I get off, so I wake him early and try to get a little play out of him but it doesn't last long before he jumps out of bed and leaves me frustrated. I jumped up and ask "Is there something wrong?" "No, why?" "I don't know you just seem distant." "I don't mean to be I just hate having this drive every weekend." "Luke, we've been over this again and again. I'm not having this discussion again. I have my work and you have yours. I'm not moving and neither are you." He grabbed me in his arms and held my head against his chest. "I know and I'm sorry I brought it up. Once I get the kids through college, everything will change." "So you keep saying." "I've gotta go baby, I love you." "I love you too." With a kiss he was gone. He usually hangs around for a while on Sunday but he had to get back to prepare for a meeting tomorrow.

I thought about the whole weekend thing with Luke and I just felt lonely. Maybe it was all the happenings, or maybe we are just too comfortable together. Oh well, I have another big day ahead and don't need to cloud my thoughts with things I can't fix right now. I ran by the pastry store and picked up my order for the day. Thank goodness I don't have to do this every time I open the store. It's getting rather expensive. Harriet and Cheryl were already going through inventory when I arrived and said "It's about time you got here, we're starving!" "Well if I had known we had an eight o:clock meeting I would have rushed!" We all laugh and I open the pastry boxes. The coffee is hot and the pastries are yummy. It's gonna be a good day.

It was not only a good day but a great one. I saw some friends I hadn't seen in quite some time. We sold a lot more than we had planned, and we had to lock the door at five because people were still coming. I really don't like doing that but it had been one hell of a week and I was beat. We finally rang up the last sale around five thirty. I told the girls to come to the back and have a glass of wine and put our feet up for a while. I got no complaints from either one. I raised my glass and said "I want to propose a toast, to the newest place in town, and the spectacular people who work there." "Here, here."

Darla Hagan

Chapter 4

Life here is pretty much the same as it was when I was young. There are more businesses in town and it has spread out a little but still your basic small town. When Julie and I were young, we spent a lot of time in the river, skiing at Canyon Lake, and playing at Jacobs Well and of course Blue Hole. There were a lot of summer activities but winters were a little boring. Weekends were usually spent in the cabin with our girlfriends talking about boys and all the things teenage girls do. I really miss those times. Then I start thinking of Julie again and my whole mood goes to hell.

Sunday was finally over. We took a quick

Coming Home

inventory, had another glass of wine, cleaned up and decided to take off Monday. "Goodnight girls. Thank you so much for the exceptional help you've been this week." "Hey girlie, it was a great opening and should be a big hit from now on. Goodnight sweetie. I'll see you Tuesday." said Harriet. I crossed my fingers and said "Let's hope so." I drove home listening to the radio playing Stand By Me. The moon was bright and the night was cool. I rolled down my window and it felt so good. I stopped by the grocery store and picked up something from the deli and another bottle of wine. It's gonna be a long crazy night. I am feeling everything is going to come down on me when I get home. I drive past the rubble to the cabin and slowly get out feeling the weight of the week deep in my being. I reach the porch, sit down and just let it go. The tears and anguish all spill out and I scream at the night sky. "Why? Why all at once? I miss Mom and Dad. I want my sister. Damn it I hate sitting here like a blubbering fool." I dry my face, grab my bottle, take off my shoes and walk in the cool grass down to the river. I sit on the pier and stick my feet in the cold water. I unscrew the lid on the wine, thinking when did they start putting screw tops on again? I turn the bottle up and take a good long drink. I can't keep my feet in any longer. The water is too cold so I tuck them under me and take in the night I don't know if it was the wine or the cool but a comfort came over me and I felt at peace for a moment. There was a rustling of leaves from the wind and a cold chill ran down my spine. I could almost hear Daddy telling me "Everything's gonna be all right."

I pick myself up and grab the bottle of wine. Walking back to the cabin felt cooler and I run to the porch, get my food and go inside with a shiver. It felt good inside and I shook off the cool. I got a tray for my lap, turned on the TV, and planned on eating, then drinking myself into another place and time. The phone rang and I knew it was Luke. I didn't feel like talking so I let the machine pick up. He said the usual. "It's me call me when you get the message. Love you." I kept eating, drinking and clicking through channels. The wine was going down easy and my mood went from anguish to mellow. After I poured the third and final glass, I picked up the phone and called Luke. "Hi babe." "Where were you? I was worried." I lied and said I was in the shower. "You made it home safe and sound I guess." "Yeah it took a little longer due to an accident on the other side of Round Rock. The traffic was really backed up." "I'm sorry." "Would you mind if I don't come down next weekend? I mean it's a long way to drive and then I only get a few hours with you." "I understand and once the shop is up and running, I'll be able to be here on one of the days of the weekend. It's just that I feel I need to be there right now to get my name and reputation established." "I know all that and it's fine. I'm just gonna maybe come every other weekend for a while." "I'll miss you but I understand. I love you and it will get better." "Me too, night hon." "Goodnight."

That was very strange. Luke is usually tearing

Coming Home

up the road to get here. Maybe it's just a phase. I'm probably reading too much into it. So much has gone on in this past week that I don't know which way is up. I finish the wine, skip the shower and go straight to bed. I fall asleep quickly but wake up around two and can't get back to sleep. I toss and turn till the sheets are coming off the bed. I finally sit up in bed, scream and get up. I hate when I can't sleep! I always end up in the refrigerator and that's bad. I'm sitting in my kitchen with a half a gallon of milk in one hand and a brownie in the other. "Oh this can't be good!" I put away the milk and my brain said "throw the brownie away" but my hand crammed it in my mouth. Damn, now I need more milk!

I slept till eleven and did not feel bad about it at all. The sun was high in the sky but I didn't care. Everything I need to do today could be done from home in my big T-shirt, panties, and bare feet. I will call my friend John who knows everything there is to know about clearing, cleaning, building, and removing things. If he can't do it, he knows who can. Coffee gotta have coffee. The pot is dirty from yesterday morning. Luke must have forgotten to clean it. I rinse it, fill it, and turn it on. I then stumble to the bathroom to pee and brush my teeth. I catch a glance of myself in the mirror, make a face, and move on. The coffee is ready when I get back to the kitchen and it smells like Heaven. I pour a cup, pop a bagel in the toaster oven and get out my phone list.

"J and B construction John speaking." "Hi John

its Abby Laurence. "I was wondering when I was gonna hear from you." "Yeah, it's been crazy. When can you come out and talk with me?" "How about tomorrow afternoon, say two o:clock." "That will be fine, Thanks John." "See you tomorrow." That's one more step out of the way. I think for now I am just going to have it all cleared and then decide what I will do later. Maybe I'll just stay in this little cabin forever. No, that would never work. Where would I put Tessa and my someday grandchildren when they come to visit? I would like to build the new house just like the old one but it would never be the same. I thought about the shop and decided we had plenty of time to restock and straighten things on Wednesday, so I called Harriet and told her we weren't going in until then. She said she would let Cheryl know.

I'm just so tired of thinking about it all. I wish Julie was here. When we were young we always worked out our problems together. Now I don't even know where she is, what she looks like. Is her hair still short and strangely colored or has she gone back to blonde? Is she happy, is her husband a good man. So many things I would like to know but obviously never will. I took my second cup of coffee and a blanket out to the porch swing. It is so nice breathing the fresh air and listening to the river as it races its way to the sea. It is a gorgeous morning, well afternoon by now, and I just want to sit here and do nothing. Two deer walk to the edge of the woods across the river. Their ears are tuned in to any unusual noises and their ever watchful eyes are making sure it's safe to come out. They get a

Coming Home

whiff of human and look in my direction to see if I am a threat. I stay very still and they finally decide to walk down the hill and get a cool drink from the river. They are one of nature's most beautiful creatures. I understand hunting for food but hunting to hang a head with horns on the wall leaves me with less than a warm fuzzy feeling.

John calls and says he can come out now if I have the time. I tell him to come on, then run to put some real clothes on, much to my dismay. This is good, they can get started sooner and I won't have to see the reminders every day. I make some fresh sweet tea and wait. When he arrives I offer tea but he said "maybe after we look around." We walk up the hill and he is scribbling on a clip board. "Do you want to keep the slab?" "No, the only thing I would like to save is the fireplace. Is it possible to break it down?" "It won't be easy but with it being cut stones, we can do the best we can." "Thank you, John, everything else can go. Try to save as many trees as possible but if they have to go I understand." "Is there anything in here you want to keep?" "Only if you find something you think is salvageable and I would like." "Okay, Abby, I've got what I need. Let's go have that tea and talk about it."

I poured two glasses, and we sat at the kitchen table. "Tearing apart the fireplace will take some time but the rest should only take about a week. We have to break up the slab, pull out the beams and try to do all of this without bothering the landscape too much."

"When do you think you can get started?" "I've got the guys on a job that should be finished by the end of the week, so maybe we could get started as soon as next Monday." "Oh John, that would be great. The sooner the better." "It's a hard thing that happened to you Abby. You seem to be handling it well." "Trust me, if it wasn't for opening the shop and keeping so busy I think I would be a total basket case!" "Well, you hang in there kiddo, and we'll take good care of you." "I knew you would. Thanks so much John." "Thanks for the tea Abby, we'll see you next week." "Goodbye, John thanks again."

My heart fell when he left, just knowing it was coming to a real end. I call Luke and he answers "Hi hon everything okay?" "No, I just talked with John. They are going to start demolition next week." "That's a good thing, right?" Yes but it's depressing." "Look babe, I'm really sorry but I am swamped, can we talk later?" "Sure." I said confused. "Thanks, love you." "Yeah, bye." "Well that really helped, so glad I called." I know I shouldn't take it out on him but damn it I really need him right now. Okay enough of that, I think I'll do some laundry, and maybe rearrange some furniture. I need to do something or I'll just sit in this big ole pity pool!

When Luke finally called I was really pissed about our earlier conversation and wouldn't even answer the phone. He left the same message and I just clicked the TV to another channel and stared at the blinking light on the phone. Two hours later he called

Coming Home

back. This time I was in the tub and just listened. "Hey it's me, pick up. I know you're there Abby. I'm sorry but I was really in a bind when you called. Call me when you get ready. I love you." I don't doubt that he loves me. I just don't feel like going over everything again. I didn't call back and fell asleep quickly.

The night before caught up to me I guess. The week went by fast and the weekend was another busy one. We did have Cheryl but it wasn't crazy, just busy. I finally called Luke Wednesday evening. "Hey." "Well it took two days to miss me?" "No, it took two days to gather my courage." "You know better than that, I love you Abby and I should have been there for you." "They start tearing the place apart Monday. I think I will ride in to Austin and buy a few things for the shop." "I will be down Friday. Is there any way I can have you all day?" "Not this week, it's going to take a while before I am comfortable enough to hire a new person." "Oh well, I'll take what I can get." "I love you Luke, Nite." "Goodnight hon." I really do miss him and am looking forward to Friday.

I decided to look at some of the pictures that were salvaged. Oh my, there's Mom in her apron in the kitchen. That was a very common sight. Here's Julie and me in the back yard spraying each other with the water hose, and Dad fishing off the pier. So many memories. I am so happy to, at least, have something left. Something shiny caught my eye and I dug down to the bottom to find a key. It is probably one of Julie's journal keys. She wrote about everything and kept all of it under lock and key. I just put it back and decided to go on to bed. It was enough for one day.

The crew woke me up Monday morning hauling in equipment and unloading large machinery. I got up made coffee, put on a smidgen of make-up, an adorable skirt from the shop with my inlay-ed cowboy boots. It was a little cool so I added a scarf to the mix. I poured a to go cup of coffee and left for Austin.

On my way to the city, I remembered how much I hated the traffic and opted for the outlet mall in San Marcos instead. I could spend an entire day there and still not cover everything. My first stop was the paper and ribbon store. I can get tissue paper in large quantities to wrap jewelry and such in at the shop. I also picked up some nice paper bags, to use on the lower end pieces. I have special ones with the name of the shop, The Yellow Rose, on them that I use for the higher end items or for my best customers. I also picked up some different size boxes for small things. I usually order all these things but I'm here so why not pick up a few.

I spent the rest of the day shopping for myself. I bought some new undies, shoes, a new outfit, and even had a manicure and pedicure. I was ready to go home. It had been a full day and I needed to stop by the shop and drop off the items, and go to the grocery store so I will have some food in the house. It was nice to be in the shop alone. I could take it all in and moved a few things around after I put away my packages. Good

Coming Home

grief food is outrageous. One hundred and fifty four dollars and I don't feel like I could eat on what I bought for more than two days, of course three bottles of wine didn't help any!

It was almost dark when I arrived home and I could see that the house was down. There were no walls at all, just a huge rock fireplace and a pile of debris. Everyone was gone and all the machinery sat silent. I just drove past and tried not to think about it. I saw the light blinking on the phone when I walked in and decided to wait until I put up my groceries to tackle the calls. My ice cream was just at that perfect softness you get when it's starting to melt so I had to open it and sample a few bites. I got everything put away and went to the phone. You have three messages, beep- "Hey hon, I know you were going to Austin but give me a call when you get home, love you." Beep. "Hey girlie, I got a call from the supplier and our shipment will be here Wednesday around ten am. Give me a call if you want me to meet you." Beep "Hey Abby, its John, Uh we're gonna wait to tackle that fireplace last. I want everything cleared first. I think it will make things easier. Talk to you tomorrow, Bye." I called Harriet first and told her she didn't have to come, that I could take care of it but I might as well have talked to my hand. "Child, what else do I have to do? You wouldn't deny an old lady her only pleasure now would you?" "You are such a bad liar. I'll see you tomorrow."

I took a quick shower, put on my jammies, poured a glass of wine and called Luke... "Hi babe."

Darla Hagan

"Hey, how was your day?" "You wouldn't believe the amount of paperwork I have on my desk! How was your shopping?" "Good actually, I bought some things for the shop, and some cute little undies just for you." "I can't wait to see them." "Do you think you'll be here by seven?" "I'm going to try like hell." "Wanna go out Saturday to Blair House for a nice meal and come home and see what pops up?" "Ooh I think something just stirred right now!" "Ha, good I'll see you Friday, love you." "You too, Goodnight."

Harriet was of course already at the shop when I arrived. She had coffee brewing and I brought some orange cranberry scones. We were both early so we sat and talked while we ate and drank our coffee. How are you Hon? I mean really?" "I'm doing okay. Thank goodness for this shop and you to keep me busy. I went to the outlet yesterday and picked up a few things." "Good I was thinking we might make a display of the higher end boots up where you see them when you walk in the door." "That would be great. We can move that old chair from the back with one of our long stand up mirrors so they can try them on right there. People walking by will be able to see them and that might draw them in. I wish I could get you in a pair!" "Are you kidding? Not with these bunion feet!" We both laugh and hear a knock on the back door. "Delivery." "It looks like playtime is over!" "I'm excited to see the new things. I'm coming." I yell as I am walking to the door.

We unloaded, stocked the shelves and display

cases, and put away the over stock. Once again we are ready for business. Next week I think we'll mark down some items that don't seem to be moving, I think to myself as I say "Goodbye" to Harriet and drive to the cabin. They have begun hauling away the debris and started breaking up the concrete. It looks like a bigger mess today than yesterday. Everyone was gone and the machinery sat quiet.

Darla Hagan

Chapter 5

  Thursday wasn't busy but steady. It gave me time to catch up on the books and ponder what was going on sale next week. I pulled a few things and put them on a rack in the back, then continued to do that throughout the day. Friday came and I am really excited to see Luke. The day was busy and before I know it, it was two o:clock. My cell phone rang and it was John. "Uh, Abby this is John." "Hi John, what's up?" "We have a bit of a situation out here. Is there any way you can come out right now?" "We're pretty busy John. Is it that important?" "Yes ma'am, it very important." "Now you're scaring me John." "Just come out as soon as you can." "Okay I'll be there shortly." I was staring into space and Harriet asks "Abby, are you okay?" "That was John. Something's happened at the house and he said I needed to be there right away." "Then go child. I can handle these people. They can wait if they need too." "Uh, okay, I'll hurry back."

I got my purse and scurried out the back door. What in the hell could be that important that couldn't wait until Monday? I turned into the drive and there were police cars, fire rescue, and a coroner van sitting there. "Oh my God, what the hell?" I stopped the car and got out with a perplexed look on my face. John came walking toward me with a policeman in tow. "John, what's going on, why are all these people here?" "Abby this is officer Langley." He looked more like someone's baby boy than a police officer but I put my hand out. "Nice to meet you ma'am. Ma'am, do you know any reason why there would be a body buried under your slab?" A wave of darkness crossed before me and I stumbled. John steadied me before I fell. "What? What kind of body?" "Human, ma'am." I look at John and ask "Who is it?" "I was kinda hoping you could tell me that ma'am." I am stunned to say the least and words just will not come out of my mouth. "The body was wrapped in plastic bags with no identification. It is hard to tell until we do an autopsy to find the cause of death. Hopefully we can come up with dental records or something. I am afraid this has become a crime scene and no further work can be done until the case has been investigated." "I understand. I suppose there is no way to know how long that will take?" "It could take days, it could take weeks.

Ms. Laurence, do you have any idea who would have done this?" "No, that part of the house is not that old. John, didn't your crew do the work?" "Yes ma'am but the body was under the re-bar. Someone went to a lot of trouble to make that happen." "So it wasn't there before you set the re-bar?" "Nope, we dug down and poured new dirt. Once the new dirt was in the re-bar went on top of that." "When was that approximately?" Officer Langley asked. "It was about ten months ago." He said, "We poured the slab, then took another three months to finish the room." I spoke softly " They never even had a chance to furnish the room before they died", Officer Langley asked "How did your parents die?" "They swerved to miss a deer and lost control of the car. It happened on Devil's Backbone about 5 months ago." "I'm sorry for your loss ma'am. Can you think of any reason they might do this?" "Absolutely not! They were the kindest people I know. The whole town came out for the funeral." "I just have to ask ma'am. I'm sorry, and I will let you know when we find out something. For now, sit tight and don't leave town." "Does this make me a suspect?" "At this point, everyone's a suspect." With a tip of his hat he was gone. I looked at John and said "What the hell, John? Who would bury a body under our house?" "People do crazy things Abby. We will move our equipment out next week and you can let us know when everything has settled down." "Come to the cabin and let me pay you what I owe you up till now."

Coming Home

John was pulling out of the drive when Luke was coming in. "Hey babe, who was that?" "That's John, my contractor. Luke something awful has happened." He took me in his arms and said "What? What's wrong?" "They found a body under the concrete floor of the sun room." "What?" We sat down on the steps of the cabin and he ask "Who is it?" "They don't know. They will have to do an autopsy and whatever else they do in these situations." "Do you have any idea who it could be? Have there been any missing persons reports as of late?" "I haven't the slightest clue. Oh, Luke, am I just cursed? Why do these things keep happening?" He holds me closer and rubs my shoulder. "A body, a freaking body! Why would anyone do that to my Daddy? Do people just look for an opportunity and take advantage? Who would kill someone and bury them under all that wire? Do you think someone planned this around pouring that slab?"

I looked out toward the river trying to absorb everything I just heard. Then I snapped back and said "Dinner, Oh my gosh Luke I'm so sorry." "No, no shh" He held me and said "It's okay, I'm sure you've got something we can scrape together. "Come on inside and we'll do just that." "I need to call Harriet. She will be wondering why I didn't come back." I dialed the number and she answered on the first ring. "Are you alright? I've been worried sick!" I explained the situation and told her we could talk more about it tomorrow.

Darla Hagan

Luke made us some sandwiches and a beer. We ate in silence, both seemingly in deep thought. We watched a little TV and went to bed. So much for our big night of hot sex!

I couldn't sleep, just lie in bed thinking. Finally sleep came and I woke to the smell of peppers, and onions. I walked up behind Luke and said "That smells wonderful." He turned around and said "Hey there sleepy head." "Apparently everything is working on my stress levels more than I thought." "Are you hungry?" "I'm starving." "Good, sit my lady and I shall feed you." I laughed as he put the tea towel over his arm like a waiter and served me. "Bon Appetite." He said and kissed the top of my head. "Oh baby, this is perfect." He had made a frittata with peppers, onions, and cheese and laid it all on a bed of crispy hash browns. "You always know what I need. I love you." "Me too, now let's eat before it gets cold."

"Harriet's niece is going to be in town again next weekend and I thought I might take off on Saturday and Sunday." "Oh man, I've got a client who couldn't come in during the week and I agreed to meet him Saturday." "Can't you change it to the next week?" "It was a real challenge making it work that weekend. I'm, sorry babe." "Well if it can't be, it can't be. I'll just work and let Cheryl help me change things around. It's good to keep the displays changing." I ate my food but was no longer interested in it. When we finished I cleaned the dishes and took a shower, got dressed and kissed Luke on the way out. When I got home he was

Coming Home

watching sports so I gave him a hello kiss, got a book and went to the bedroom to read. Around eight Luke came in and said "I wondered what happened to you." I just smiled as he walked to the bathroom and thought, yeah you were so worried it took over an hour to check on me! I fixed dinner and we ate in front of the TV. When it came time for bed, I went in and turned out the lights. When Luke came in I pretended to be asleep. I barely stirred when he got into bed and I heard him sigh very deeply and turn to face the wall. I know I shouldn't be that way but it's been a very stressful couple of days and I just don't feel like dealing with anything at this moment.

I awoke to some nibbling on my pleasure spots. I completely forgot I was upset and gave into the feelings. With one hand on my breast and another working between my legs, it was hard to concentrate on anything. There was a very warm tongue doing some magic on my neck and earlobes. "Mmmm" I said as I turned over to face him. "You sure know how to make someone forget their worries. "That was the plan." I actually felt a little more passion and urgency to our lovemaking. Maybe being apart every other weekend is working after all.

I dressed for work and Luke lay in bed watching me. "You're certainly being lazy this morning." "I'm just enjoying the view." I smiled and wiggled my ass when I left the room. I didn't have to look to know he was smiling, which in turn, made me smile. When I went in to kiss him goodbye, I made it a long lingering one. I got up to go and he tried to keep me from leaving. I slipped from his grip and smiled as I walked out the door. I blew him a kiss and told him "I love you and will see you in two weeks."

On the drive I was thinking about the weekend we could have if Luke didn't have to work so hard. I stopped and bought some pastries and Harriet had the coffee ready when I arrived. There were fewer customers than usual and that gave us time to get things in order for the next week . When the weather is good enough to be on the lake, the traffic slows. My friend Ann came in and we talked for a good while. She told me of a party she was having next Saturday and begged me to come. I told her no, that I had to much to do right now. She said as she was leaving "Think about it and come on by." I said "Thanks Ann but probably not."

I talked with Luke and he apologized again about not being able to come next weekend. I said "That's okay babe, we'll have plenty of other weekends." But in my heart I did not mean it. We said goodnight I took a shower and crashed.

I decided not go to the shop on Monday. I guess I just wanted to sit and wallow in my own self pity. There was still no word on the body so nothing can be moved until they complete their investigation. I just moped around in my pajamas all day, washing a load of clothes, and very little else. When Luke called, I told him I had a bad headache and didn't really feel

Coming Home

like talking so the conversation was short.

I went in Tuesday and rearranged a few things, restocked inventory, looked at new things, and ordered some new jewelry pieces. When Saturday came I was ready for something besides work. The closer to closing the more I thought about Ann's party the more inclined I was to go. I finally decided what the hell and drove home to change.

When I arrived it was hard to find a place to park. I almost decided to go back home but something pulled at me and I parked. I sat for a minute watching people on the patio and then made my way into the house.

There were people everywhere and I knew most all of them. It was like old home week. Someone put a drink in my hand and the party began. I saw so many people I hadn't seen in years and loved visiting with all of them. I was standing by the fireplace when someone whispered in my ear "Hello Ms. Laurence." Startled, I turned to see Cade Tate standing beside me with a huge grin on his face.." "Hi, how are you?" "I'm good and you? I heard about your new problems with your place." "Yeah, sucks to be me, and it's kind of creepy." Damn I had forgotten how nice looking he was. "Do they know any more about the body?" "No, and I'm just stuck until they tell me I can start working on the place again." I forgot how blue his eyes were against that dark hair. "How do you know Ann?" We went to the same youth group as kids. Someone decided it would be fun after all these years to get back together, so here we are. It's amazing how many of us still live in or close to the area." "That would explain the people here that I don't know." "Yeah that goes the same for me with all the locals." "Where do you live?" "Crystal City." Ann had a huge deck that over looked the river, complete with a full bar and DJ. There were a few people dancing, others sitting and telling the tales of their lives since they last saw each other. I ask "Do you dance?" "Yes ma'am" and held out his hand with a smile. I took it and we fell into step on the dance floor. "You're very smooth Mr. Tate." "Why thank you ma'am, as are you."

I held him at a reasonable distance but he sure felt good in my arms. Luke would be spitting nails about now but Luke's not here and Cade is. The song was over and I thanked him and went over to talk to Ann. "Oh Abby, I am so glad you're here. Are you having a good time?" "Yes, this is a very nice distraction. I got another glass of wine and walked over to some other friends to sit and chat.

The DJ played Last Date by Floyd Cranmer and I didn't have to look far to find Cade. "I love this song, let's dance." I all but dragged him to the dance floor. The wine had begun to mellow me so I danced a little closer than I should but it just felt so damn good, and he smelled heavenly. I wanted to just bury myself in him. The song stopped and so did he. I took his hand and said "Let's go for a walk:. "Okay." We walked down the steps to the river's edge. The sounds of the night

Coming Home

and the wine made me very bold and I looked up at him. I touched his cheek with the back of my fingers, then stood on my tip toes to kiss him. It was a great kiss and when I pushed my tongue past his teeth, I realized what I was doing and pulled away. "We better get back to the party." I started up the hill and he caught me by the hand and pulled me in close looked into my eyes and then kissed me deeply and with a passion like I have not felt since I was so in love with Jimmy. I melted into to him and then came to my senses. I pulled away and started up the hill back to the house. I really enjoyed the encounter, maybe too much, what the hell, way too much. I knew I had to get out of there before I made a complete fool of myself. I looked for Ann to let her know I was leaving. There was a group of people around a guy playing guitar and singing silly songs and she begged me to stay. I told her thanks for inviting me, I enjoyed myself very much. "But I really need to get home. I'm sorry but I have a killer headache. I guess I have just been out of the loop too long!" As she walked me to the door she said "I am so glad you came and you know I will be hitting you up for the fundraiser again this year." "I will be happy to do whatever I can. Come see me soon. Oh wait, maybe it will be better when things calm down!" We hugged and said "Goodnight." I talked to myself all the way home. "What the hell is the matter with you Abigail? Where the hell was his wife? What were you thinking?"

Sunday was slow at the shop so I decided to go home. Harriet said she and Cheryl had it covered. I thought about the night before and felt foolish. I called Luke and asked how the meeting went. He said "It was worth staying in town for even though I haven't quite reeled the client in yet, it looks promising. How was your evening?" "Oh it was Okay. I saw some friends I hadn't seen in a while, and I always enjoy Ann. Will I see you next week?" "Yes ma-am. I miss my girl!" "Good, I miss my guy. You have a good rest of the day and I love you." "I love you too, goodbye."

    I put the phone on the railing of the porch and sat back in the swing looking out at the view. The phone buzzed and I thought Luke had forgotten to tell me something. I didn't recognize the number and pulled up the message. It was from Cade. "I enjoyed last evening." I text back "The pleasure was all mine." Good grief why did I say that? I don't need to lead this man on. Maybe that will be the last of it.

    I decided to go back to the shop after and it was bustling with customers. I scolded Harriet for not calling me and she just mumbled something and kept waiting on a customer. The rest of the day flew by and I was once again on my way home. The phone was ringing when I walked in the door and I grabbed it and said "Hi." It was Luke, which I was pretty sure it would be, and he was in a very good mood. He told me he was staying until Monday this weekend so maybe I could take off Sunday and we could have at least one full day together. That sounded so good. I miss him and this thing with Cade just makes me miss him more.

Coming Home

Later that evening I was looking at Facebook and noticed Ann had written to thank everyone for making the party so much fun. She said it was nice to have Abby and Luke there as well. Just a slip I guess. A few minutes later I receive a text again from that unknown number. "What the hell, Abby and Luke? I don't remember any Luke being there. It was me you were kissing. Did I pick up the wrong signals or is she just trying to protect you?" I text back "No, you picked up the right signals, they are just at the wrong time, and yes she probably was trying to protect me." I would rather call and talk to you about this. I will call this evening." Damn it, what have I done? It just felt so good in the moment and now I have a mess on my hands!

When I called he answered a very stern "Hello." I said "Cade I'm sorry, you're a great guy and I enjoyed our moment together very much but I am very involved with Luke. He's having problems with his divorce and still has two kids in college. I just can't leave that. If this had all happened at a different time, it might have turned out differently for both of us but again, wrong place, wrong time." "I understand. Goodbye Abby." "Goodbye Cade." He had already hung up before I finished saying goodbye. I felt better getting that settled, after all the man is married! A few minutes later my phone beeped again and I read "I understand but that doesn't mean I have to like it." I didn't reply.

I decided to go back to the shop after and it was bustling with customers. I scolded Harriet for not calling me and she just mumbled something and kept waiting on a customer. The rest of the day flew by and I was once again on my way home. The phone was ringing when I walked in the door and I grabbed it and said "Hi." It was Luke, which I was pretty sure it would be, and he was in a very good mood. He told me he was staying until Monday this weekend so maybe I could take off Sunday and we could have at least one full day together. That sounded so good. I miss him and this thing with Cade just makes me miss him more.

The week went quickly but the sales were down and still no word on the body. I'm really getting used to the small cabin and enjoy coming home to the sounds of the river and wind in the trees. Even though the weather is a lot cooler, my front porch is still my sanctuary. I just use more blankets. Monday was not going to work for Luke so he will be here a day early instead. I'm going to grab a quick shower and fix a little snack tray with some wine. He can shower when he gets here and maybe I can persuade him to cuddle in the hammock with me. I'll put a heavy quilt on the bottom to keep the cool air from hitting us from the bottom. I can work on that while he is showering.

I just finished the snack tray when I see Luke's car lights coming down the drive. Perfect timing. I meet him at the door with a huge passionate kiss and glass of wine. "Whoa, if I had known I was going to get this welcome I would have taken off early!" I just smiled and took his duffel bag to the closet. "I thought since it was such a mild night we might lie in the hammock for a while. Maybe we can build a fire in the pit and watch it till it dies down." I said between kisses all over his neck and face. "Mmm, you keep that up and we won't make it to the hammock." I gave him a shove toward the bedroom and said "Go ahead and shower and I'll get things ready." I slapped his bottom, winked and sashayed out of the room with a huge grin on my face.

I already had the wood in the pit and soaked it with charcoal starter. One match and we would have an excellent fire to watch as we snacked, drank, and swung in the hammock. For some reason things felt different. They were more comfortable and I felt very close to Luke. We had finished the snacks and I was uncorking a second bottle when I see car lights coming down the drive. "Who the hell could that be at this hour?"

Darla Hagan

Chapter 6

I sat the bottle down and saw the emblem on the car. It was the Sheriff. He stopped the car and got out. He started towards the door, tipped his hat and said "nice fire." "Thanks. What brings you out Dean?" "Well Abby, we found out who the body is." "Really? Well, who is it?" With a strange look on his face he said "It's your ex-husband Jimmy Laurence!" "What?" Suddenly my balance was off and my head was spinning in all directions. When I found my voice I said "How can it be Jimmy? He's in New York and I can't even remember the last time I heard from him. "The findings are about as accurate as they can be. With DNA and dental records, we are 99% sure it's

Coming Home

Jimmy." We made some calls and he just left work one day and never showed back up. I asked them if they didn't think that was a little unusual and they told me he did that kind of thing all the time. "But why would he be here? He knew my parents wouldn't have anything to do with him and Tessa is in San Marcos." "Well I was kinda hoping you could shed some light on that. When was the last time you had any contact with Jimmy?" I really had to think and finally said, "It has been at least six years." "Did your parents ever say anything about him coming by anytime?" "No, Dean, you know how much they disliked him after the divorce. You don't think they had something to do with this do you?" "Now Abby, I've known your parents all my life but the questions have to be asked. I would like to talk to Tessa. You can call her and let her know what's happening and set up a time to come and talk to me. Don't worry Abby we will get this all figured out." "Thanks, Dean." "You should be able to start on your house soon. I'll talk with you tomorrow when everything settles down a little." "Thanks, Dean." I hugged him and he said "Goodnight Abby, Luke. Oh and you probably know this but don't plan on leaving town for a while." He tipped his hat and walked to his car.

I looked at Luke, who was now sitting beside me holding my hand and rubbing it. "How Luke, why? Why would he be here?" "Babe, I have no idea." "Never in my wildest dreams would I have guessed Jimmy! Jimmy!" "I know Abby, it's crazy. He didn't have any contact with your parents that you know of?"

"No, Luke, like I said there was no love lost between him and my parents. He would have no reason to be here." "Well, the police are on it and I'm sure they will come up with something soon. Let's put out the fire and go to bed. I'm worn out." "Okay Luke. You put it out and I will gather everything else." I couldn't help but think about what just happened. After all these years, why would Jimmy show up at my parents house, and end up under it!"

I crawled into bed but couldn't sleep. Luke was snoring before his head hit the pillow. I finally got up and went to the kitchen for a drink of water. I stared out the window at the space they found him and tried to come up with some sort of rhyme or reason as to why Jimmy would be here. Maybe he was dying and wanted to leave a will for Tessa. Ha, no way he would do that. He'd give it to charity before he'd let her have it. Maybe he was dying and feeling remorse, no that doesn't fly either. What then? What could the reason possibly be? I poured the water out of the glass and went back to bed but sleep came in spurts. I was afraid I would keep Luke awake so I went to the couch.

I slept but kept having the same dream of Jimmy's hand coming out of the ground, so it was not restful to say the least. I called Harriet to see if by some chance Cheryl was in town and thankfully she is. I give Harriet a quick run down of what had taken place last night and she said "Don't you worry about a thing honey, we'll take care of the shop. You just take care of yourself."

Coming Home

Luke comes sleepily walking into the kitchen. He puts his arms around me and asked if I got any sleep at all? I lied and said "yeah, I just didn't want to bother you in case I couldn't." "You really shouldn't worry about all this. It has nothing to do with you." "How can you say that? Jimmy was buried under my parents house! My parents died in a horrible accident. It's all too strange Luke. Why would Jimmy be here with them? Why would he be here at all?" "I don't know but let the police worry about it." "Really Luke, I'm suppose to just go on my merry way without a care in the world when my ex husband, whom I haven't seen or heard from in years is found under my parents house in a trash bag, really!"

I turned and walked out into the cool air of the morning. The chill hit me but I didn't care. My head was swimming from all the different reasons I was trying to come up with for all of this. Luke walked out and I just put my hand up and said "Not now Luke." He turned and went back in the house. I just stood on the porch staring at nothing, hearing nothing, feeling nothing. The phone rang and I heard Luke telling the other party he would get me. "It's the Sheriff." I looked at him and took the phone from him. "Hello, Dean. What can I do for you?" "I'm sorry to tell you this but the construction will have to wait a bit longer. Forensics and the crime scene investigators want to do some more probing." "Dean at this point I don't care if they dig up the whole damn place." "Now Abby, I know this is hard but we will be working on this every minute possible." "I know you will. I'm sorry, I'm just upset and tired. I know you will do everything you can to make things happen." "You let us worry about all this and you take care of you." "Okay, thanks." "Goodbye Abby." "Goodbye Dean."

Luke took me by the shoulders and lead me back into the house. I told him I was going in and try to take a nap. He kissed my forehead looked me in the eyes and said "it's gonna be okay hon, its's gonna be okay." I just shook my head and went to the bedroom.

I had never really talked about Jimmy to Luke other than we were married and divorced without communication other than child support checks. I never went into much more than that. The fact that he abandoned us and wanted nothing to do with our child was just too hard to say.

"I can't sleep so I think I will go to the shop Luke I need to keep busy." "I will probably have a lot of questions but I think that is just what I need. "Are you sure babe? Would you like for me to come and run interference for you?" "No I'll be fine. I might as well take the heat now and get it over with. It's not going anywhere and the questions will be coming anyway." "You do what you think is best but I will be here if you need me." I hugged him and said "Oh Luke, I don't know what I would do without you." "Well you don't have to worry about that. I'm not going anywhere. I think I'll call the office and stay a couple more days." "No, Luke that is not necessary, really I will be fine." He hugged me tightly and said "I love you babe. Now

Coming Home

go get 'em!" He turned me around and slapped my bottom. It was a refreshing gesture from all the bad that had been happening and I smiled as I walked to my car.

It was business as usual and lots of gossip and speculation. I just shook my head, smiled and moved on to the next person. I sat down for a bite to eat and to work on my books just to get out of the main stream for a while. Harriet is very good at running interference. I checked my phone and to my surprise I had a message from Cade. "Heard the news. Anything I can do?" What in the world makes him think he can do anything? I text back "That's very sweet but I am fine." Ding! "Well let me know if you change your mind."

The day was finally over and I headed home to Luke. He met me at the door with a kiss and long hug. "How'd it go today." "It was Okay. I hid out in the storeroom working on my books for a long time. How was your day?" "Boring without you. Are you hungry?" "Yes I am." "Good, I made your favorite pasta, Chicken Sophia from that little Mediterranean Restaurant we like so much in Bastrop." "You are the best Luke. Let me wash up and I will be ready." I kissed him and went off to the bathroom.

"When I come out I'll set the table and throw together some garlic bread." "That's all taken care of." "Okay, then I will get the wine." I said as I came from the bathroom drying my hands. "That's done too. All you have to do is sit down and eat." We ate in silence and retired to the living room. "Luke, you don't think

Mom and Dad had anything to do with this?" "Why would you even consider that Abby?" "I don't know. It's just odd that Dad built the sun room the way he did, and that's where Jimmy was. I mean I haven't heard from him in years. The last support check was when Tessa turned eighteen. Then he started sending money for college but that was just checks mailed through the courts. I'm still not sure why he did that but was very grateful that he did. "Abby, let's go to bed and try to get you relaxed a little . Come on, I'll rub your back."

The back rub lasted all of thirty seconds and Luke was sound asleep. I slipped out of bed, grabbed a blanket off the couch and went out to the swing. I really need to call Julie and let her know what's going on even though the police have not ask me about her. I am sure they will want to talk to her with questions about Mom and Dad. I'll try her tomorrow. I know she won't pick up but at least I can leave a voice mail. She won't have a clue about any of it but I guess I should at least give her a heads up. I am sure they will want to know about my relationship before and after the marriage. Not having her with me during the divorce only added to my grief. I was getting chilled so I went back to bed and fell into a restless sleep filled with strange dreams.

I awoke to complete silence and it startled me for a minute. I realized I was in an empty bed. I sleepily got up and walked to the living room. The front door was open but the windowed storm door was closed. Luke was standing down by the water's edge.

Coming Home

He had his hands in his pockets and was just staring motionless. Not wanting to disturb his thoughts, I went in the kitchen and began making coffee. While the coffee was brewing I started preparations for my day. I was applying my last bit of mascara when I heard Luke come in.

The news of Jimmy's remains had not hit the gossip train as of yet, because things were rather quiet with mostly tourist and very few townspeople. I heard my phone ding to tell me I had a message but was busy and forgot about it till I was in my car ready to go home. I pulled the phone from my purse and hit message. It was from Cade! "If you need someone to talk to I'm here." That's very sweet but maybe a little out of line, I thought to myself but no harm in saying Thank You. I text-ed back "Sorry I didn't get your message till now. I'm fine, thank you for being so sweet." I put the phone back in my purse, dug out my keys and it dinged again. "I'm here anytime you need me." Okay, that's too much. I will not answer that one.

The ride home was peaceful and Luke had a fire going and wonderful aromas coming from the kitchen. He met me at the door with a kiss and helped me off with my coat. "It smells like heaven in here." "Dinner's ready, just keeping warm in the oven. Would you like to shower or have a nice long bath before we eat?" "That would be wonderful." He helped me off with my boots and I headed for the bathroom. I opted for a shower so I could wash my hair. I could hear him setting the table and moving around in the kitchen and it made me smile.

The shower was refreshing and I called out to Luke as I was walking toward the kitchen "Would you mind if I wear my robe to dinner?" "I would love for you to wear your robe for dinner." He kissed me peeked down my robe and pulled out my chair. "Thank you kind sir." "Anything for my lady." We made small talk and ate, cleared the dishes, and decided to watch a movie. My mind was not on the movie at all. I was still trying to find a connection to Jimmy and my parents. Maybe they called him to talk about Tessa's future, or maybe they had connections with him all this time and I did not know. No, there's no way, they hated Jimmy. They would never have him in their home willingly. Maybe he needed money and came to Daddy. No, Jimmy would never do that. I know he had some criminal cases that didn't turn out the way they wanted. Maybe he came here to hide and one of them found him. That's absolutely crazy. This is the last place he would come. There has got to be something I'm missing. What can it be?

The movie was over and Luke was in a very affectionate mood. We went to bed and made love. My mind not really in to what was happening but did not let Luke know. I praised him on his performance in an out of breath tone. That will work every time! We lay there a minute before Luke got up and brought me a towel. I cleaned up the wetness of our lovemaking and cuddled until he fell asleep.

Chapter 7

Sunday the store was filled with every local gossip, and a few I didn't even know. "Oh Abby, I'm so sorry. First your parents, now this" "Abby, I heard. What has this world come to?" "Abby, do you know why?" It went on like that all day. I just smiled, shook my head, and helped the next customer. I thought the day would never end. Harriet tried her best to run interference but there were just too many. I personally escorted Mrs. Vouyant out the door while she was talking and said "Thanks for your concern Clara. Come back and see us real soon." I then shut the door and locked it before anyone else could sneak in. "Whew, that was very sneaky there Abby but effective." We both broke out laughing. I put my arm around her shoulder and said "Go home Harriet. You have more than earned your worth today. I'll come in tomorrow or maybe Tuesday to straighten up." "Okay, honey. I hate to admit it but I am pooped. I'll see you Tuesday." I locked the money and receipts in the safe, turned out the lights, locked the back door, sat in my car and drew a deep breathe of relief. I found a bottle of my favorite wine on the table with a note that said nothing more than "I love you." I retrieved a glass, a corkscrew, and filled the glass. I kicked off my boots, propped up some pillows, grabbed a blanket and leaned back on the couch. I took a long drink and then decided I needed a fire. I put a fire log on the bottom of the grated then covered it with logs and lit it. In a few minutes I had a pretty good fire going. I got back in my position on the couch and thought how it was just like Luke to leave me the wine. He is so thoughtful and caring most of the time. The lovemaking just lacks sparks, fireworks, and that push me up against the wall kind of passion.

The combination of the long day and the wine hit me and I was ready for bed. I took a quick shower and the phone was blinking when I came out, so I knew Luke had called and I didn't even hear it ring! I stumbled to the bed and fell in wearing just my underwear. I forgot to pee and knew I would wake up in an hour and have to go so, I dragged myself out of bed and made my way back to the bathroom.

I called Luke right away when I woke up to

Coming Home

apologize for not answering and he said "No problem, I've got a client, I'll talk to you later." He hung up before I could even say thank you for the wine. I just lay there staring at the phone with my mouth open. "What the hell just happen? Has our relationship come to this? Oh never mind, I have more things to think about than my petty insecurities.

    I crawled out of bed, put on coffee and got in the shower. The aroma of the coffee and the shower worked their magic to wake me. I didn't realize until I looked at the clock , it was after eleven! The cell phone rang and I picked it up to see who it was. "Ann? What does she want? Hello." "Hey Abby, it's Ann." "Hi Ann, what's up?" "I was calling to see if you are going to help me out again this year with the fund raiser? I know you have a lot going on but maybe this will help take your mind off some things." I usually come down this time of year and help her because it's a worthy cause. "What have you assigned me to do this year?" "The seating arrangements. You know better than anyone, who hates who, who has to be right up front, and who needs to be closest to the bar. I have the list and the table layout that I can email to you." "I would be happy to help Ann." "I don't want to add to your problems and I can always find someone to do it, though they would never be as good as you." "I'll do it, Ann. It will be a good project for me." "Will Luke be attending?" "It depends on the weekend." "I'll just add his name and you can work it from there. I will get this together and email it as soon as I can. I am looking forward to this event. I think it will be our best one yet." "I'll be looking for your email." "Great, I am so excited. Thank you Abby, and you know I am really sorry about everything that's going on. Love you." "Love you too. Bye."

When I hung up the phone I noticed out the kitchen window, the sheriff was standing in the rubble of concrete. I watched him as he picked up something, looked at it, then threw it back down. He stared off into the trees, shook his head and turned to walk back to his car. He drove out of the drive and my mind began to wander again and I started to fall back into that dark hole. "No!" I shouted. "I'm not going there again." I took my coffee to the bathroom and prepared myself for what was left of the day.

I got Ann's email around three, printed out the layout and names, then sat at the table to do a quick review of names. I was already getting an idea of some of the no's, okay's, and definitely nots, when I came across a name with a note beside it stating, no date, put at our table. It was Cade Tate. "Oh great, now I have to share a table with a man that is clearly interested in me and that I have a hard time being around. Where the hell is his wife? He's got that something that pulls me in. I check the calendar and see that the event is scheduled when Luke will be in Colorado with his fishing buddies for their annual get together. I threw the list down and got a glass of wine. "I know it's early but I don't care." As if someone was listening.

Now I can't get my mind off Cade Tate. The

Coming Home

way he smelled, the way he filled out his jeans, the feel of his arms around me when we danced. I just had a tingle run from the pit of my stomach to my toes. I shook my head and came out of the daze I was in. " Whew, I gotta do something else for a while. l will wash my sheets or something. I stripped the beds and washed everything including blankets. During the down time I shined the mirrors. When the washer would stop, I would put those clothes in the dryer and another in the washer. I cleaned my bathroom from top to bottom and put another load in the washer. When I finished one bathroom I went to the other and started a new load of clothes. When all was finished I was making the beds when the phone rang. It was Luke! "Hi Hon, what's wrong?" "Why would something be wrong?" "Well it's so early. You usually don't call early unless something is wrong." "Babe, it's six thirty and I am already home!" "Oh my goodness! I have been cleaning all day and didn't realize it was that late, How was your day?" "Apparently not as busy as yours. I just noticed on the calendar that your big fund raiser is the same weekend as my trip with the guys." "Yeah, Ann called and sent over the seating arrangement chart. That's all she's ask me to do so far." "Are you okay with me not going?" "I'd really rather you be there but I know how much this trip means to you and I wouldn't ask you to change your plans just for that." "You're the best-est girlfriend in the whole world. I'll make it up to you." "I'll start a list." We both laughed, said I love you and Goodnight.

I disconnected and started to think about going

somewhere myself, I could go see Tessa but at her age I just seem to be in the way. She would never tell me, but I remember being that age and having your parents around. I have a friend from Houston who owns a Condo in Reno, Maybe I'll give her a call and see if we can get together and catch up on old times and new.

I was still in an energetic mood and decided to start looking at the table seating layout again. I wrote everyones name on a piece of paper and started placing them here and there. Each round table holds eight and it was going well until I took another look and noticed I had the Smithers and Vouyants at the same table. They are like the Hatfields and McCoys, so that will never do. I can just see it now. One of them would walk out and they are both huge contributors. One would always try to outdo the other, which is good for us but having them together would be a disaster. I'll trade one of them to an equally good table. Suzanne always co-chairs with Ann so she and her husband Dean, the sheriff, the mayor and his wife, Ann and whoever she's dating this week, and Cade and I will be at the head table.

I got everyone where I wanted them and emailed it back to Ann for final approval. I was going to suggest using tiny picture frames to put the names in, and have them engraved with the logo and the year but decided that would be an unnecessary expense and chose to just go with the usual paper. I ask her to let me know if anyone needed moving and to double check spellings of names. I don't want to offend anyone,

Coming Home

especially when they are donating big money. We have a really good group of men that play for the evening and donate their time as long as we feed them. It was after ten and I grabbed a bite to eat , a shower and hit the bed.

Harriet was already busy as can be when I arrived at the shop Tuesday morning. I didn't make coffee at home, and was very happy to smell it brewing when I walked in the door. "Morning Darlin', there's scones in there with the coffee." "Harriet you are the best." "I know baby but don't tell my husband. He'll expect the same thing at home!" We both laughed and she turned and went back to straightening clothes. "I'm going to work on the books for a while, then I'll come out and help. We have to start thinking about what to purchase for Christmas. I don't want to go overboard. I would rather have too little than too much." I heard Harriet yell from the front of the store. "Sounds good to me."

It took most of the morning to finish up the bookwork and I am amazed but quite happy at how well the shop is doing. I walked across the street and bought lunch for us and told Harriet to sit and put her feet up for a while. We were chatting about this and that when I brought up leaving for a week. She said "I think that would be fantastic honey. Where are you and Luke thinking about going?" "Actually it will just be me. Luke will be on his annual trip with the guys. I was thinking of having Kelsie meet me in Reno." "That would be perfect. It would get you out of this mess for a while and you could talk about old times. When are you planning this?" "I'm thinking after Ann's big fund raiser, in about two weeks. Do you think Cheryl would be willing to work?" "She told me anytime we needed her, just call. I'll check with her tonight." We finished lunch and got the shop in shape for Thursday. If we continue to do this well I will think about hiring someone to help during the Christmas season and maybe continue afterward. It's hard to find someone who wants to work every weekend. College students usually work out. Maybe I can hire two and they can trade off. Cheryl is awesome but newly retired and I hate to keep calling on her, even though she does like to make extra money now and then.

I stopped by the store on the way home for groceries, and picked up what I needed for the place cards. I put everything away, got a bite to eat and sat down at the computer. I checked all my emails before going to Ann's. She had made a couple of changes which I agreed with and changed spelling on three people. I want to get through with them and I have tomorrow to take my time preparing them for the printer. Luke called and we chatted for a while. He had a very good day and was sharing every last boring detail with me! I finally said "Honey, I'm beat. I'm gonna take a shower and go to bed." I wasn't tired at all. I just didn't want to hear anymore about work. Selfish? Maybe but I'm just not in the mood. I'm ready to get on with the table arrangements. We said "I love you and Goodnight."

Coming Home

I made a new seating template, then began putting names on each one, I double checked the place settings as I was going. Ann had placed the mayor and his wife, Suzanne and Dean, Ann and John, and me and Cade Tate at the head table. Just seeing his name made me tingle in places I shouldn't. I finished typing in all the names, printed it out, then started on the place card list. I couldn't decide if I should put them in alphabetical order or by table. I went with by table. I will be the one placing them and I will have an easier time doing it that way. I emailed the final draft to Ann for her approval and got ready for bed.

I could not keep Cade out of my dreams. I would wake up and go back to sleep only to start a new one. It was becoming very frustrating and I finally just got up and made coffee. I went out on the porch bundled up in a blanket just as the sun was showing me a new day. I tried to clear my mind of everything and just take it all in but Cade kept sneaking back in. Why is he doing this to me. I am perfectly happy with Luke. It has to have something to do with the passion. Maybe somewhere in my little pea brain it's telling me that I need that. Hell, Cade may not have a passionate bone in his body! I really don't believe that because of the way I felt dancing with him. It just seems like he would be a very good lover. Damn it, there I go again. I have got to get dressed and go to the printer to finish this table arrangement mess.

I quickly grabbed everything and headed out. After dropping off everything and answering any last minute questions, the printer and I were happy. I decided to run get my dry cleaning and ran into Cheryl. She was so excited and told me "I am so happy you asked me to work. I needed a little extra money for Christmas. Do not hesitate to call me anytime." "I assured her I wouldn't and thanked her for her enthusiasm. It made me feel a lot better about leaving. I could enjoy myself without having to worry about my shop. It was at that moment I realized I needed a new dress for the occasion. Tomorrow I will see what I have at the shop and if I don't find anything that suits me, I will go shopping next week. I think I will put on my sweats later and take a run. I have been a little lax in that department as of late.

It was a great day and I could not wait to talk with Luke. I did however talk with Kelsie earlier about the condo and she is way to busy to get away but talked me into going anyway. I am a big girl. I can do this by myself. It might be a little lonely but then again I like to have time to myself. I can see the countryside and maybe do a little gambling. I will go online later and see what entertainment they have that weekend. Maybe I'll take in a show or two. Now I am getting excited. I better go online and book my flight and rental car. Oh, now I can't wait!

Chapter 8

The weeks went by quickly and I found the perfect outfit for the event in my shop. A strapless short dress with a sheer jacket that flows when I walk. Some strappy high heel sandals with just enough sparkle to make them stand out. I had my hair done up and hope to wow everyone there. Hopefully they will be so impressed with how I look they won't worry about gossip. Yeah, right.

I put on the finishing touches, slipped into my shoes, grabbed the place cards, and left for the hall. Ann was there giving last minute instructions to everyone and I began placing the cards. "Oh, Abby, thank you so much for this. You know I couldn't do this without you." "Oh Ann, you could do this with one hand tied behind your back. You are the best event planner on the planet." Just then one of the chefs walked up and said the oven was giving them problems. Ann just threw her hands up, rolled her eyes at me and followed quickly behind him. I just laughed and continued with my chore. It took about an hour, as I had expected and I had just finished when the first people started to arrive. I quickly went to the restroom to freshen up. When I came out, there were more, so I got a glass of wine from the bar and headed to my table.

Oh my God, he's there and he's watching me as I am walking toward him. He has a smile that would melt any woman's heart. When I reached the table, he rose from his chair and pulled out mine. "I do believe you are seated right here ma'am." I smiled and said "Why Mr. Tate, I do believe you're right." "May I say for the record Ms. Laurance. You look lovely." "Thank you, Mr. Tate. You clean up pretty good yourself." He laughed and we sat down just as a waiter came by to ask if we required anything. "I'll have another red wine, please." "I'll have crown and coke" said Cade. "So, how are things coming with your house?" "Very slowly I'm afraid. They won't let me do anything until they have completed their investigation." "I'm really sorry to hear about all that. Do they have any ideas." "None, as of yet. It has been a real mystery to all of us." Finally someone else at our table. The small talk was getting very uncomfortable for me. "Good evening Mayor, Mrs. Mayor." We laughed and

Coming Home

I hugged Carol and introduced Cade to the both of them. Suzanne was following Ann around so Dean just came and sat at the table with us.

Everyone has been seated and Ann starts the ceremony with her saying "I want to thank everyone for attending and the silent auction is happening in the front room." She also thanked all of the volunteers who donated their time and to the businesses that donated items for the auctions. "We are about to begin serving the wonderful meal our fabulous caterers have prepared for us, then we will start the live auction. Everyone sit back, relax, enjoy your meal, and don't forget the open bar."

She came back to the table and all the men stood while her friend pulled out her chair. The caterers knew to begin when she was seated and the servers were prompt. Within fifteen minutes everyone had their meal. The room was alive with chatter and clinking of silverware. There was a lot of small talk at our table. Then Cade and I began our on conversation.

I learned that Cade had no children. He has a Chocolate Lab name Thor that he gave to his wife right before they found out she was ill. "He never left her side and in the end he put his paw on her hand and whimpered as if he knew." I touched his hand and said "Oh Cade, I'm so sorry." "He moped around for a month. He would barely eat and spent most of his time in her room. I thought I was going to lose him too but one morning when I stopped by the room to check on him, I felt a very strong feeling, like there was someone or something there. Since that time he stopped going to the room, started eating again, and is a much happier dog." "What about you? How are you coping with everything." "It took longer for me. I was on the couch one evening, feeling sorry for myself of course, and Thor lifted his head and and started barking at nothing. I tried to figure out what had him so stirred up and suddenly a calmness came over me, like the weight I had been carrying around just lifted and I was at peace. It was very spiritual." I had chill bumps and tears by now and he reached over to wipe one away with his thumb. That small gesture brought a whole new feeling in my heart for this man. To have been through the heartbreak of losing your soul mate must be the most devastating thing one could have happen. We were drawn from our conversation to the sound of Ann's voice over the microphone. Now it all made sense. The reason he never mentioned his wife and why he was always alone.

She announced the silent auction would end at ten o:clock and the live auction would begin in about twenty minutes. "So grab a drink and your wallet and get ready." Cade extended his hand and asked "Would you like to check out the silent auction?" "Actually I would." I took his hand as he pulled out my chair and then put my hand in the bend of his arm" We said hellos along the way and I tried to avoid making a big deal of being on someone else's arm beside Lukes. I'm sure the rumor mill will be crazy by morning. I really didn't care because I was off for the next week heading

Coming Home

to Reno on Monday. A whole week to myself! I can't wait. The boots I had donated were already double the price, and the rhinestone belt was doing just as well. "It is so great when a community comes together like this and gives generously to a worthy cause." I said to Cade and then saw something. "Oh my goodness. This handbag is a must have. I am going to bid on it." Cade was interested in a trip to the Caribbean and was bidding on it. "We'll have to be sure and check back before ten to re-bid if necessary. I'll set the alarm on my watch so we don't forget." "That's a great idea Mr. Tate. It sounds like the live auction is starting up. Maybe we should head back to our table." "After you Ms. Laurance." There were more looks and whispers as we made our way back to the table.

The auction was crazy. Everyone was bidding like they had money to burn. When it was over Ann had a smile on her face you couldn't have wiped off with sand paper. She thanked everyone extensively and the room was suddenly filled with music. Couples began to dance and mingle. "Would you like something from the bar?" "Yes, I would love a glass of Cabernet." "I'll be right back." I watched as he walked away as did every other woman in the room. Ann was by my side just filled with joy over how everything was going. She said "Cade's a dream isn't he? He has been such a recluse since his wife died. It's great to see him smiling and enjoying himself." I excused myself and went to the ladies room. What am I doing? I could just eat him up! My mind was running a mile a minute and some of my thoughts made me blush. I was putting the finishing touches on my lipstick when Mindy Mosher strolled in. Oh hell, here we go. I thought to myself. "Why Abby Laurance, don't you look lovely this evening? Of course who wouldn't on the arm of Cade Tate?" "He's just my table mate, Mindy. Luke is on a trip this week and Ann had to fill the table." "Uh Hum." She said as she checked her hair. "It was nice seeing you Mindy. Enjoy your evening." I quickly exited the room and made my way back to the table.

Cade was waiting with my glass of wine and stood to pull out my chair. "Where did you run off too? We missed the ten o:clock deadline. I'm afraid someone over bid you on your handbag." "That's okay. I'm sure someone else will enjoy it just as much and I would." I took a sip of the wine and it was amazing. "This is very good. Did you happen to notice where it is from?" "Somewhere in the Kerville area. You know they have about thirty wineries in and around there. I've recently seen tour buses that take people to the wineries and Luckenbach." "Well, it's very good. I will have to check it out before I leave for the evening. I didn't ask. Did you get your trip?" "Nope, someone hit it at nine fifty nine." "I hate when that happens."

The band was in full swing and the dance floor was full. I love watching couples that have danced together for years. They just seem to know what the other is thinking before the next move. They just seem to flow flawlessly across the floor. The music was mostly country with a few older rock and roll tunes. Of course there are also the belly rubbing songs like The

Coming Home

Way You Look Tonight. They began playing He'll Have To Go and I was lost in the song when I felt Cade's hand in mine and asking " Would you do me the honor of dancing with me?" "Why I'd love too."

I tried to make small talk so I could keep from staring into those big blue eyes. "I used to skate to this song when I was a little girl." "No kidding? I used to go skating a lot when I was young." Turns out our skating rinks were within twenty miles of each other. His was a very large one in the city and mine was a Mom and Pop place in the country. I had actually been to the large one and did not like it. "It just proves what a small world it really can be." The song was over and I was clapping and turning to go back to my seat when Cade took my hand and pulled me closer to dance to the next song. "Do you mind?" "No, not at all. I love to dance." I could feel his smoothly shaven cheek on my mine and it felt quite good. He smelled heavenly and between the dancing and the wine I was feeling way too comfortable in his arms. None of this mattered because I didn't plan on leaving them anytime soon!

We did go back to the table, mingling along the way and he refreshed our drinks. I was already feeling that warm glow that wine gives me and had hoped the meal would have curbed those senses but I was feeling good and it was going down easy. After all they are small glasses!

Here I am sitting at a table of my friends and all I can think about is jumping right in the middle of this guy, throwing him to the floor, and stripping him naked! "What? Oh I am sorry. I was in deep thought." "I asked if you would like to dance?" "Yes" I said as I blushed down to my toes. "I'd love to." The later the evening got, the closer the dancing. I believe at one point I was actually nibbling on his ear! He feels so good. I've got to get a grip on myself. I've got Luke and I love Luke and oh there's that breath on my neck again. I am losing control and need to snap back into reality and get out of here before I do something I will regret.

When we returned to the table I picked up my bag and told everyone how much I enjoyed the evening. I congratulated Ann on another job well done. I turned to Cade and thanked him for a lovely evening as I was picking up my pashmina. "Now what kind of a gentleman would I be if I didn't walk you to your car?" I smiled knowing I was not going to get out of it and he helped me with my things. He opened the car door for me and I went to kiss him on the cheek but he took me in his arms and kissed me long and sweet. I thought I was going to melt into a pool at his feet. I knew I had to get out of there quickly, so I got in the car, said "Goodnight", and drove away.

I rolled down the windows and took in the fresh cool air to somehow bring me out of my stupor and drive the few miles to my cabin. When I got inside. I came out of my clothes, brushed my teeth and hit the bed.

Coming Home

I was awakened to a door slamming shut, and a vehicle driving away. I got out of bed and went to the front door to peek out and saw Cade's truck leaving. I turned around and leaned against the door. Thank goodness I didn't hear him earlier. Surely he didn't think last night meant anything. He knows about Luke and our relationship. I opened the door only to find a package with a note that read I wanted to make sure you got this. I really enjoyed the evening. It was signed "Cade" I opened the package to find a bottle of wine and the bag that I had bid on. I knew then that this had to stop. I text-ed him and said "You shouldn't have done this but Thank You." He text-ed back "A lovely gift for a lovely lady." I did not reply. Instead, I started packing. It seemed really important to get out of town now more than ever.

Darla Hagan

Chapter 9

When I landed I rented a car and drove to my sanctuary for the next week. I had to get the key from the manager and made my way to the condo. It is gorgeous here this time of year even though it's cold. The trees are not like they are in the east with all the pretty colors but in the upper elevations there is a slight blanket of snow covering the Sierra Nevada Mountains and it is breath taking. I had called ahead to the manager and asked him to turn on the heat and the water heater. When I walked into the Great room, there was a fire glowing in the fireplace and it gave me a warm cozy feeling. I said to myself. "I will be on that couch with a glass of wine as soon as I get everything

Coming Home

done."

I brought in my things and put them away in the bedroom, took a quick shower, and dressed to go to the store for supplies. Every time I come here I am mesmerized by the beauty of it all. We usually come in the summer months so the mountains are bare of snow. It is refreshing to be here when they look like they have a fluffy white blanket on them. The temperature is mild, maybe forty or so with the sun shining. It makes for a perfect change from the one hundred degree summer we just had. I feel great. This is going to be a good week.

I was getting in my rental when my phone dinged letting me know I had a message. I figured it was Luke and checked it out. It was Cade! I hope you enjoyed your evening as much as I did." "This has got to stop." I text-ed "We need to talk. I will call you later." I continued to the store and got provisions for the week. The sun was going down and it was cooling off pretty quickly. When I got back to the condo, the fire felt great.

Just as I promised myself, I had my jammies on and a glass of wine on the way. I replenished the wood in the fireplace, and by the time I made a snack, and poured the wine, it was in full blaze. It never ceases to amaze me how a fire can just put you into a complete state of relaxation. I had another glass of wine. Now I might have the courage to call Cade and tell him to back off.

Darla Hagan

I got my phone, dialed his number, and waited for an answer. "Hello, Pretty Lady." "Cade, we have been over this before. You are a great guy and I did enjoy myself but I am in a relationship. Yes, I lead you on. That is my fault and I apolgize but there are too many complications involved. Maybe if this had happened at a different time in my life, it would be right but now is the wrong time." "It's okay Abby. I really do understand and I commend you for being so honest again but you must understand my confusion." "Goodbye Cade." "Goodbye Abby." I disconnected and closed my eyes. I could smell him and feel his sweet breath on my neck. I just threw the phone on the coffee table and let out a big sigh.

The wine and the day had caught up with me and I fell asleep cozied up on the couch. I woke up and felt like I would pee in my pants if I didn't get up right now! I made my way to the bathroom and then hit the bed.

I woke to another beautiful day and decided to work on the computer looking for Christmas items for the store. The Great room has windows floor to ceiling opened to the second floor. It has a perfect view of the town and the mountains. I looked through inventory from some of my suppliers and found some really unusual things, and a few traditional things. I got a lot ordered and hopefully will have them by December. I need to call Harriet but I don't want her to think I am checking up on her. I haven't heard a word from Luke but that's not unusual because they are almost always in

Coming Home

a non cell phone area.

I can't stop myself from thinking about Cade and the way I feel in his arms. I know it's just that "what you can't have" thing. He's just having his first crush after his wife died. I don't want to be a rebound but I just have a feeling for him that I don't feel with Luke. I love Luke and don't want to give up our relationship. After being so in love with Jimmy and having it ripped away I don't think I can ever have a complete relationship again. I like it long distance. I like having my freedom and not having to come home and cook dinner and how was your day and blah blah blah. Luke understands this and we work well as a couple. There may not be the I can't wait to get you to bed so we will do it right here on the floor kind of thing but there's so much more to a relationship than that. Can a person have both? Jimmy and I did. We were a lot younger then and maybe that's the reason.

The day went well and I got some great things ordered. I ate a sandwich and decided I would clean up and go to the casino. I can get something for dinner and gamble a little. I went on line to see if anyone I like was having a show and came up empty. I took my time getting ready and decided to wear a dress and heels. I don't know but it seems people are nicer to you when you look nice. I pulled into the parking garage at Harrah's and had valet take my car. I started out with a little PaiGow and moved on to the slots. I was up about a hundred dollars when my stomach started telling me it was hungry. I went to the steak house at Harrah's and had a salad, a petite filet mignon topped with crab meat in a Bearnaise sauce. I even had room for cheesecake. I like this place because it is consistently good. I decided I had had enough of the smoke and the noise and went back to the condo.

I took a shower to get the smoke off my body and out of my hair, put on my jammies, grabbed a glass of wine and planted myself on the couch in front of the fire. Thank Goodness for natural gas, cause I can have a blaze in no time. It has been such a relaxing day. I think I will drink myself to sleep again!

I woke up around six, still not used to the two hour time difference, put on some sweats and tennis shoes for a run before breakfast. It was a little nippy this morning but once I got going I warmed up. I stretched for a few minutes and started off down the hill. When I reached the bottom I was totally out of breath. I always forget about the altitude difference. Even though I live in the hill country it's nothing compared to these higher elevations. I decided to walk back up the hill. Tomorrow I will take it a little slower. I made breakfast and was a complete slug the rest of the day. I called Kelsie to tell her what she was missing and how much I appreciated her letting me do this. She said "I'm coming in the day after you leave, darn it. I could really use some Abby, Kelsie time. Maybe next year. Love you lots bye." "Me too, Bye."

The week went by way too quickly and I was headed home. I talked to Luke last night and the fellas

Coming Home

had a good trip. Apparently we will be eating fish and venison a lot this year! I dropped off the rental car and headed for my boarding area. The airport was bustling with tourist, some hoping for good snow on the mountain, others ready to shove their money into slot machines hoping for that big win. I went through security and settled in to wait for my flight. I watched a young mother wrestling with her small son trying to keep him entertained. A flight across from me had just landed and everyone was full of laughter. Some old, some young, couples holding hands and looking so much in love. Some looking like they couldn't stand the sight of each other and are here for a quick divorce, others looking like they may have slipped away for a little rendezvous. Hmm.. I could see sneaking away to meet a lover. Maybe Cade Tate. Oh my gosh where did that come from? That's just ridiculous but it would be fun! I just had a tingle low in the belly and I am sure I am blushing from head to toe. I look at the gentleman beside me and he smiles just like he knows what I was thinking. I smile back and turn away. I got up to get a bottle of water to take on the plane. Canned water tastes awful and unless you're in first class that's what you get! I made that mistake once, and never again will I board an airplane without a bottle of water.

They called my flight to board and I gather my things and boarding pass. I get in line with everyone else and make my way to the plane. I have an assigned seat so there's no rush to get there. A young man with an I pad and ear buds smiles at me then leans back to relax and enjoy the ride. We go through the usual safety spiel and turn off all electronic devices, etc, etc. Once in the air the young man goes back into his coma and I pull out my book reader and begin to read.

The flight was uneventful and although I had stops, I didn't have to change planes and was more than ready to see Austin, Texas come into view. My luggage came quickly and I took a shuttle to my car. The weather was mild for November but that is part of Texas charm. It can be 75 at noon and 35 at two o:clock. Today was not windy and lots of sunshine making 60 degrees feel really good.

I called Harriet and she told me they had a pretty good week and everything I needed was in the safe. "How was your trip?" "It was very relaxing. Thanks again so much for keeping the store open." "Oh nonsense, you know I would be lost without that store." I got in some Christmas things you must have ordered and just put them in the large storage room." "Wow that was quick delivery. I'll have to remember them next year." "Okay honey you get home and settle in. We'll see you on Wednesday." You're an angel." "Yes, I know!"

Instead of going home I went by the shop and got the money and receipts from the safe. I would need something to do other than putting away my things. I wouldn't see Luke till Friday and I was really missing him.

I checked my messages after I got everything unloaded. There were a couple of telemarketers, some

Coming Home

friends just calling to chat, and one from John telling me he got the okay from the police to continue demolition on the property. "Just give me a call when you are ready and I will set up a schedule." "I can't believe it! I can actually get on with my life. I wonder if they found the truth about Jimmy and why he was here? No, someone would have called me. I'll call John tomorrow and get things going again. "Maybe my life will be somewhat back to normal!" I deleted all the messages and called Luke. "Hi baby. Have you come down off you high yet?" "Oh, Abby, this had to be the best trip ever. I love you for being so understanding about these trips." "You know I trust you with all my heart and you can go with your buds anytime you want. Except that Steve guy. I'm not sure I trust him." I laughed. Steve's been married and divorced four times. He's like a chick magnet and where there's one chick there's two or three! "You know I don't mess with Steve." "I'm teasing you babe but just in case you get any ideas I'm coming for Steve's hide!" Luke just laughed. "It's good to hear your voice baby." "You too. Friday seems like a long way off." "It will be here before you know it. I don't suppose you could get Saturday off?" "I would not feel right doing that after being gone for a week." "I knew that but thought I would try anyway." "I love you babe. I'm gonna work on getting myself and my clothes back together. Talk to you tomorrow?" "Absolutely. I love you too. You sleep well." "You too. Goodnight."

I decided to wait on unpacking and took a shower and wrapped in a blanket instead. I went out and crawled in my hammock to listen to the river and look at the stars. It was a beautiful clear night and very cool. It felt good to be home. To smell the familiar smells and listen to the familiar sounds of the woods. The moon shining just bright enough not to mask the millions of stars in the night sky. At times like these I am content to just continue living in the cabin but I will be happy to have a real house again. If nothing else it will be nice not to have the mess of broken concrete and dirt. That poor lonely chimney and fireplace standing stately in the rubble. "Don't worry, we're gonna give you a home again." Okay, I am talking to chimneys. Time for bed."

I was having one of those dreams where the phone is ringing, and you wake up to the phone ringing! I didn't get the call because I was in a daze from trying to wake up and make sense out of what was happening. When I heard someone leaving a message I finally realized what was going on. Oh good grief, it's ten thirty. I must have been really tired.

I went straight for the coffee pot, then listened to the message. It was Luke telling me his project for Monday was canceled and he could stay an extra day. That is so cool. We haven't had a whole day together in forever. I think we will just stay in bed all day There is suppose to be a cold front coming through on 'Saturday and temperatures are suppose to be in the thirties. Sounds like cuddle time.

I got my coffee, my computer, my phone and set

Coming Home

up shop on the kitchen table. First order of business was to get my books, and bank deposits done. Harriet was right. They did have a good week. I will have to place a new order soon to replenish inventory. With Thanksgiving coming there will be new people in town. That means more business. Thank goodness I only have one day off. If I didn't, I'd have to spend Thanksgiving day with Luke and his family. I love his kids and all but his Mother drives me crazy. "When are you two gonna get married. It's just not right living the way you do. Blah, Blah, Blah." Tessa called and asked if she would be a terrible daughter if she spent Thanksgiving break with her boyfriend in Dallas. I will miss having her here but knew this day would come soon. I told her to enjoy herself and maybe next year we can have everyone in the new house. "You're the best, Mom. I love you." "You just be careful and have fun. I love you too."

I finished the deposit and was quite impressed. I will drop it off at the bank later. Next order of business was to call John. I dialed the number and heard "J & B construction, John here." "Hi John, it's Abby." "Hey kiddo, how was your vacation?" "It was so quiet and peaceful. I almost forgot I had worries here at home. When can you get started again?" "Well, with Thanksgiving in a week, I'm gonna have to say the Monday after." "That will be fine John. Did the police say anything about Jimmy?" "Not a word, just said they had all the evidence they needed so I could continue when you gave the go-ahead." "Okay then. I'll see you on Monday after Thanksgiving."

"Yes ma'am, we'll be there. Goodbye Abby and welcome back." I said thanks and hung up.

Chapter 10

I got out the plans for the house just to refresh my memory. I don't think I will put the sun porch back on. Maybe I could make room for it on the back of the house with a large deck and fire pit. Yeah that would be good. On posts not concrete! It could have different levels that go down the slope towards the river. I need to get with the architect and re-work the plans. I had originally wanted to replace it just as it was but after spending time at the condo I am having second thoughts. Having a Great Room with all those windows overlooking the deck and the river and all the wildlife would be so good for the soul. "I'm going to call right now." He answered and said he was available this evening around six. I said "that would be great. Would you like to eat while we are brainstorming?" "Sure, I never turn down food. Brandy is going out with friends and I was going to have to fix my own or grab something." "Okay, I'll see you at six." I am actually getting excited now about things. Now I have to get in the kitchen and cook-up something. A bag of tortellini, some sauce and garlic bread. Viola, I'm good to go. I should straighten the house a little, and unpack my suitcases. I should have time for at least two loads of clothes, and a quick shower before he arrives. Dinner will be a snap.

Denny Baxter is probably one of the best home builders in the State of Texas. He costs more but he pays attention to detail. We went to school together. He was a couple of years ahead of me, and his wife is the same age. They have one child the same age as Tessa so we have known each other for years.

I finished my shower, the laundry, and have dinner warming when Denny knocks on the door. I hugged him and ask "Do you want to eat first and then get down to business?" "The way it smells in here, I don't believe I could think without eating!" "All Right then. Have a seat and I'll open some wine. Chianti okay?" "Chianti is perfect." I got the wine and a corkscrew and handed it to him while I was getting the place settings. I put the tortellini in a bowl and garlic bread in a basket. I had grated some Parmesan cheese and got it from the fridge. I also poured two glasses of ice water. I brought everything to the table and we

Coming Home

toasted "To your new home." "Thank you. I have some new ideas I want to run by you and get your view on them." " Sounds good. This is delicious Abby." "Thanks Denny." If he only knew how very simple it was to make!

    I put the dishes in the dishwasher as Denny was laying plans on the table. "I'm going in a completely different direction from the first plans. I want a Great room that's all glass facing the River. Then maybe a deck that steps down the slope but big. I want it as wide as the Great room, with a fire pit right in the middle of it." "Whoa, slow down Abby. I can't keep up!" We laughed and I sat down at the table. "Here are some house plan books, and also deck plans. Take a look through them while I try to take all this down." "Okay, sorry. I'm just excited to finally get started on all of this." I looked through one of the books and didn't see anything that stood out, so I picked up another one. "What if we go with this plan, make the kitchen a little larger, put the laundry room over here, and maybe when we rebuild the fireplace we could expand it some. I know we would have to use more stone but maybe there's a way to do it without showing new from old." "That will be up to John, he's the stone guy. I can make the other changes and talk with John to incorporate the fireplace." "Great, now what about this deck plan?" He took the book and walked out to look at the slope down to the river. "I think if we do it just right with the levels, this should work. Let me take these ideas and see what I can come up with. I'll get with John about the slope and leveling for the house." "That sounds great Denny, Thank you for being so patient with me, and be sure to tell Brandy I said Hi." He gathered his things and said "Thanks for dinner and I'll be back with you probably some time next week." "Okay, good night and drive safe." I shut the door and squeaked with excitement. "Wow, this is really happening."

The shop was bustling with early Christmas shoppers. I'm so glad I got those things in that I ordered in Reno. I'm always a last minute person so it always surprises me that people start so early. I plan on having a Saturday in the first weekend of December with food and wine and maybe ten percent off everything in the store.

Luke was in an awesome and lovable mood this weekend and it was great to have an extra day to spend with him. We talked about our trips and all the venison and fish he brought me will last for quite a while. We both decided the time away was good for us. Thanksgiving was this weekend and we would not be together again. We stayed in bed till noon on Monday before he finally decided to get on the road and go back to Temple and his world.

I spent Thanksgiving day with a turkey sandwich and getting the shop ready for the weekend. There will be lots of new people in town visiting relatives and looking for Christmas items and presents, I'm expecting lots of business. I tried to place duplicate items in the stock room easily accessible so we can replace them quickly. I will have Cheryl run the

Coming Home

register so Harriet and I can try to keep things flowing. I have stocked a lot. I hope I haven't bought too much. I don't like to keep seasonal items from year to year so I always put them on super sale the week before Christmas. The phone rang and I heard Harriet's voice asking me if I need any help. She said "The kids have eaten and gone so I'm free!" I told her "I'm just about finished. You sit and put your feet up tonight, because I'm gonna run you ragged tomorrow." "You know I love being busy." "Yes I do. You have a good relaxing evening and I will see you tomorrow." "Goodnight dear." "Goodnight."

I talked to Luke, then went to bed so I could get up early and prepare for the day. People were hovering around the door when I got there. Harriet was already there and Cheryl pulled in right beside me. We looked at each other with an Oh My Gosh expression and got out of the car. "Are you ready for this?" "I don't know. Did you see all those people?" "Yeah I did. It's a good thing I have my running boots on!" We laughed and walked in the back door to the smell of coffee and pumpkin bread. We don't open until ten and it is only nine forty so we have a few minutes to drink a cup of coffee, eat some of the delicious pumpkin bread, put money in the cash drawer and open the door. "Good Morning. Everyone come in." I said "Hello's and How do you dos" all day. I locked the door at six and it was six thirty before we got the last customer out the door. I locked the door behind her, turned around and gave out a long sigh. We all laughed and headed for the back room. I grabbed the money drawer and all the credit card receipts. "What a day." said Harriet. "Yeah and we have two more to go. Maybe Sunday everyone will be headed home and we'll have a break or two here and there." Cheryl asked "Are we going to restock anything tonight?" "I think Harriet and I kept that pretty well done throughout the day. You go on home. Thanks for your help and we'll see you in the morning." "Are you sure you don't need anything done?" "I'm sure. I am going to fix the cash drawer for tomorrow and put every thing else in an envelope in the safe. When I have that done I'm going home myself. Now you two scoot. We have another big day tomorrow." They both said good night and I locked the door behind them. I found a bottle of wine and a glass, sat back down and put my feet up. I nearly gulped the wine and poured another. I better get the drawer straight and head home and have another glass or two to get a buzz. It will put me to sleep and oh I can sure use some rest!

The rest of the weekend went quickly and just as I thought Sunday was very busy at noon when we opened but slowed to an even flow where we all had time to catch our breath. I am going to have to spend Tuesday and Wednesday doing some serious ordering. My inventory took a real hit but my profit margin is going to be off the charts! Today, Monday I am going to stay in my jammies all day and do absolutely nothing, except maybe the books and deposits.

John's crew arrived very early making enough noise to wake the dead. That pretty much took care of my sleeping in. I put a pillow over my head, turned up the fan, put the white noise machine on high but nothing would drown out the jackhammers and backhoes and what ever else they were using. I finally crawled out of bed. I looked out the window as I was making coffee at all the activity going on in my yard! There were dump trucks full of concrete debris, backhoes pushing and loading the trucks, The jackhammers breaking up what was left of the sun room. It was quite an orchestrated scene. I wanted to go back to bed but sleep was going to be impossible. I took my coffee, curled up on the couch and picked up the remote to click on the television. Nothing on but news and re-runs of Law & Order, NCIS, CSI Miami, and cartoons. Maybe I'll finish the book I've been reading.

I picked up the book from the coffee table but drifted off with the characters only they were Cade and I. We were dancing very close in the kitchen with him without a shirt and me with only his shirt on! I lingered there for a few minutes and then popped back and threw the book down like it was on fire. Why do I keep doing this? I know he would be here in a second if I ask him to but that would not be fair to him or Luke. I'm not leaving Luke. He's been too good to me and been through so much. I couldn't bear to hurt him more. Maybe I could just have Cade once or twice a year. Somewhere no one knows us. Holy Crap what am I thinking? A knock on the door made me nearly jump out of my skin. It was John. "Good morning John. Come in. Would you like a cup of coffee?" "No thanks Abby. I just wanted to know if you have your plans for the house yet. We can level up the areas that need to be." "I have Denny working on the final details. I'll give him a call and see how he's coming." "We still have a full weeks work and then we have to take down the fireplace." "Okay John, with the new plan the fireplace is going to be a little bit bigger. We will have to order more rock but I would like to have as much of the old rock showing inside the house as possible." "We can surely take care of that Abby. Just let me know so I can meet with the builder as soon as you're ready." "It's Denny Baxter. I am surprised he hasn't gotten in touch with you. He must be really busy." "It's that time of year." "Thanks John, I will get on it as soon as possible." I let him out and decided to take a run.

The noise was still going on when I returned but then again I guess I have another week of it according to John. So much for sleeping late. I took a quick shower, talked with Luke and did the receipts and deposits. Freaking awesome weekend! Well worth the extra work. I will put extra in the girls pay checks for all their hard work and time. A happy employee is a good employee, and I have two very happy ones.

Tuesday I went to the bank to make my deposit, and drove to the shop to work out what I felt I needed to replace. Christmas is four weeks away and I am running very low on some items. I made a few phone calls, pulled some items that were over three months old and put them on a sale rack that will go outside on the side walk. I don't like to keep anything longer than

Coming Home

that. If it hasn't moved by then, It's not going to. I like to keep new up to date items. If they don't move, I don't replace them. The only thing I keep longer are my boots. I have a wide selection but would like to stock more. The ones that are around more than six months go on sale and get replaced with a different kind.

I got everything done that I set out to do, and grabbed some take out on the way home. The phone was ringing as I walked in the door. I let the machine get it. "Abby, pick up." It was Luke. "Abby, call me as soon as you get the message. My father has had a heart attack and I really need to talk to you." I grabbed the phone. "I'm here baby. How bad is it?" "They took him into surgery. He has four blocked arteries and they are going to try stints but may have to open him up and do a by-pass." "Do you need me to come down?" "No just be close to the phone." "I will be right here. I love you baby and I can be there in three hours." "I know but just stay by the phone in case I need you." "I will. You take care of yourself and give the family my love. Keep me updated." "I will. I love you Abby." "I love you too Luke. Listen, it's going to be fine", "Talk to you soon." "Bye Bye." I really feel like I should be there but I won't go until he asks me.

Luke's father, PePaw, came through the surgery and was doing fine. Luke was exhausted and our conversation was pretty short and sweet. I hung up and my phone dinged with a message. I thought maybe Luke had forgotten something and pushed the buttons to find Cade's name! I pressed again to find a message stating "I'm a little drunk and thinking of you." "Oh my, should I answer? I need a glass of wine, maybe three!" Somewhere around midnight I text him back, "Next time let me know sooner and maybe we could have gotten drunk together!" Oh crap, take it back, take it back! It was too late I had already pressed send. Why do I let him get to me that way? I'm going to bed."

I fixed my coffee and threw a bagel in the toaster oven when I suddenly remembered what I had done last evening. I retrieved my phone to make sure. Sure enough there it was plain as the nose on my face. Then I thought what would it hurt to have a drink? Lay a few ground rules and let him know just where I stand on this situation. I gathered my courage and text-ed "What are you doing Sunday night?" "Other than TV, I have no plans." "Are you interested in that drink?" "Yes ma'am. Where would you like to go?" "How about my backyard? I'll meet you at Jacob's Well parking lot around eight. You can leave your truck and that way no one will be flapping their lips about your vehicle in my driveway. You like Bourbon, right?" "Yes ma'am. I will see you at eight Sunday." "I'll be there."

Coming Home

Chapter 11

I locked the doors at five o'clock sharp, sent Harriet home, and put the receipts and money in the safe. I had gone to the liquor store yesterday. I ran home and showered really quick, put on something warm. The temperature is very mild but still in the high fifties. We will need a fire in the pit. I had bought some munchies and I placed them nicely on a platter and stuck them in the fridge. I found a blanket to sit on and two more to wrap up in, then started out to the Wood creek area and wound around to the Jacob's Well parking lot. I am hoping I can talk to Cade about my relationship with Luke and how much I value it. He seems like a really nice person and has been through so much himself but then so has Luke and he loves me. I really don't know why I am doing this. It is wrong on so many levels but I am just drawn to the unknown. He got out of the truck and walked over to my SUV and got in. "Hello, pretty lady." He said as he kissed my hand. "How are you Cade?" "I'm doing pretty good right now." I removed my hand from his and turned the car around to go back to the cabin. "Why all the secrecy?" "I have a man in my life remember? I'm doing this to settle things between us." "I don't think I like where this is going." "Cade, I am so attracted to you I can't stand it." "But." "But I am devoted to Luke." "Look Abby, I haven't had any feelings for three years. What I feel for you is still up for grabs. I must admit I do have feelings but I am not here to ruin anyone's relationship. For the first time since my wife died, you made me feel like I was a man again. You actually made me feel wanted. You tell me right now if you feel we shouldn't see each other. I'll walk away and never bother you again. I think we both feel there is something between us."

I was quiet until we got to the cabin. We got out of the SUV and I told him to have a seat on the swing and I would be right back. I grabbed the blankets, glasses, and wine and handed them through the door to Cade. "Put them out by the fire pit." I went back in the cabin and got lighter fluid and matches. I took them down to the pit and asked Cade to light the wood I had placed in it earlier. I made my way back to the cabin and got the goodies from the fridge. The fire was raging when I returned and Cade had laid a blanket on the ground. "Oops, I forgot the corkscrew, be right back."

When I came back out, Cade was standing in front of the fire and I could see his outline. The square strong jaw, the perfectly shaped nose, and the broad straight shoulders. I could see the muscles pressing against his pants when he stood and walked over to the blanket. He saw me and smiled. I handed him the corkscrew and a bottle. "Would you do the honors Mr. Tate?" "I'd be happy to ma'am." He filled our glasses and I made a toast. "To new friendships." He raised his and repeated "To new friendships." I took a drink and stared at the fire. I could hear the river flowing through low hanging limbs, and rocks. The frogs were croaking and a soft breeze was playing with my hair. "This is very nice Abby and what a perfect night. There are a million stars out and with no city lights you can see them all." "Yeah, it's one of my favorite places. There are lots of memories here. Julie, my twin sister and I had many parties out here." "Holy crap, there are two of you?" I laughed. "Yes but Julie moved to California after college and I have only seen her once since then. That was at Mom and Dad's funeral." "What happened to your parents?" "They swerved to miss hitting a deer or something in the road on Devils Backbone Road, and lost control of the car. No one knows for sure but that's the way it looked at the scene." "That must have been very hard." "It's the reason I am back in Wimberley. I was already miserable without Jimmy, and it just seemed like the right thing for me to do." "And your sister? Why have you not seen her?" "When I married

Jimmy, she could not stand him. She was always telling me I could do better and when we graduated, she moved to California. Even after Jimmy and I divorced she still stayed away. I miss her so much and especially when Mom and Dad died."

I drank another glass of wine and was feeling pretty mellow so I decided I had better put some food in my stomach. "How are the house plans coming?" "We should have them finished by the end of the week. John was after me to get them going so he knows how to level the land. Denny is suppose to meet with him on Friday and they can get everything settled. While they are doing that John will be dismantling the fireplace." "Why doesn't he just demolish it?" "It was a very big part of my life growing up and I wanted to keep at least some little part of the old house. I intend to make it larger on the inside and put a fireplace in the master bedroom upstairs so I will have to have some new stone but most of the old will be visable to me inside the house." "That's very nice." He poured what was left of the bottle of wine and added "It's a good thing you brought two!"

He added to the fire and I lay back to gaze at the night sky. The stars were like diamonds sparkling everywhere. When he came back to the blanket, he did the same. "Sometimes when I would come to visit I would lie on a blanket or in my hammock and just spend hours staring into the night. It just seemed to soothe me. Oh look there goes a shooting star!" "Where." "Right there", and I pointed toward the southern sky. "Wow, I haven't seen one of those in a while. It's beautiful." I took his hand and kissed his fingers one by one and looked into those blue eyes sparkling from the flames of the fire. I pulled him toward me and our lips met. I know this is wrong but I want it so bad. The kiss tingles all the way to my toes. That old familiar tickle in the tummy and lower regions. I haven't felt this since Jimmy, and I am reminded of how much I have missed it. We pulled apart and looked at each other. I took his hand and we walked toward the cabin. He stopped me and ask. "Are you sure you want to do this?" I just looked at him and shut the door. He took me by the waist and pushed me up against the door with a kiss that would have made a whore blush. I started undoing his shirt, and he pulled mine over my head. He kissed both breasts one at a time before he unsnapped the bra and pulled it off my shoulders. He slipped a nipple between those beautiful soft lips and softly ran his warm tongue around it. Then went to the other one. I had his head in my hands and his hair felt like silk between my fingers. I was trying to catch my breath when his mouth found my again and that warm sweet tongue went exploring. Just when I thought I was going to lose my legs he lifts me off my feet and I wrap my legs around his waist. It's all very urgent and my hands are reaching for his belt and button on his jeans and his hands are caressing my breast, then he slips them under my hips to carry me toward the bedroom. I said "No, let's go to the kitchen!" He looked at me, shrugged his shoulders, and sat me on the counter. He removed his pants and I scooted out of mine as we were kissing and touching. I put my feet on the table to brace myself and looked deep into his eyes. Then he slid into me and my head went back as my eyes rolled and I lost myself in him. He was so gentle and his hands were everywhere. I almost came with just his touch. His wet kisses, caresses, and the slow rhythm of his hips meeting mine was more than I could stand. I let out sounds I didn't even know I could make. This just made him move faster until he was spent and I was in another realm. We both came back to our senses about the same time and breathlessly smiled at each other. "My my Ms. Laurence, you sure" His voice was interrupted by the phone The machine picked up and Luke's voice came on the line. "Hey babe, had a bad day and just wanted to hear your voice. I love you. Call me soon."

The mood that was so full of passion and urgency turned to silence and awkwardness. He picked me up and stood me on the floor. We stared at each other for a moment until I broke the silence by saying. "Cade, you know I have Luke, and we both know I shouldn't be doing this to him or you but I am not going to apologize or make any excuses. You just brought out something in me that has been hiding for years. I'm not leaving Luke. He's my life and you came along at the wrong time. I very much enjoyed what just happened between us but I do have to face reality. If you can live with that, so can I. If not, I guess you should leave."

I was shaking by the time I finished what I said.

Coming Home

Cade held my face tenderly in his hands and ask. "Do you care for me Abby?" Surprised by what he ask, I said "Yes Cade I do , very much but there is." He put his index finger on my lips and said "That's all that matters to me." He took me in his arms, picked me up and carried me to the bedroom. He lay me on the bed, got on his knees beside the bed and kissed me on the forehead. "The question is, can you live with it?" He got up and went out of the bedroom. I could hear him gathering his clothes and straightening out things we had toppled in the heat of the moment. There were a thousand things rushing through my head. What have I done? But it felt so good. Luke would be crushed but he doesn't have to know. Oh my, he's getting ready to leave. I can't let him go. I jumped out of bed and ran to his arms and pulled him back to my room. I said "No more talking." We lay in each others arms and I could feel his heart beating. "Cade?" "Yes." "Is this too much for you?" "I must say it is different and I am a little vulnerable right now but we just had incredible sex and it's hard to think about anything else. There's a part of my body at this moment that has drained all the blood from my brain, so it's just a bunch of mush in there!" We both laughed as I rolled over and straddled him. "Uh Oh" he said, and all the tension in the room seem to just fade away.

I had the alarm set for five so I could get Cade back to his truck. The evening was indescribable and it was hard to get out of those strong but gentle and loving arms but we managed. We were silent on the drive really not knowing what the other would say.

When we arrived at the truck Cade turned to me and said "Abby, last night was incredible and I'd be lying if I said different but I know your situation and I respect your honesty. If you need me or just want to talk, do not hesitate to call me." He kissed my hand and got out.

A tear fell down my cheek as he pulled away with a tip of his hat. I drove back home and crawled back into my bed and could smell Cade all over it. I was so tired I thankfully fell asleep right away. Then came the noise from the construction and there went my sleep. I lay there in my sweatpants and long sleeve T-shirt thinking about what happened and what comes next. The sex was phenomenal and I had feelings I had not felt in years. It was everything I thought it would be and more. Now what am I gonna do?

Coming Home

Chapter 12

The phone rang and I nearly jumped out of my skin. It was Luke. "Luke, oh Damn!" I fumbled for the phone, dropped it, and finally pulled it together to say "Hi baby." "Hey, I've been trying to get a hold of you since last night!" "I'm sorry babe. I went for a run, came home, showered, and crashed. Things just caught up with me and I pooped out. How are things with you?" "Everything that could go wrong did. I lost a major client, my water pump went out and Dad had a fall!" "Luke, no. I am so sorry I wasn't there for you. I can still come down if you would like." "No, Dad will be fine Maybe this will slow him down some and he will behave and do what the Doctors are telling him.

How are the renovations coming? I can hear a lot of noise in the background." "Hopefully by this time next week it will be a little quieter around here. At least there won't be any jackhammers and grinders and beep beep beep of things backing up." "That sounds good. Everything from yesterday doesn't seem so bad now that I have talked with you." "I am so sorry Luke. I should have been there for you." "Actually, it's better this way because I have calmed down and I was just feeling sorry for myself anyway." "Well you have every right to. I love you, Luke." "I love you too baby. I don't know what I would do without you." "Well you don't have to worry about that, I'm not going anywhere." "Talk to you tomorrow?" "You can count on it. Goodbye babe." "Goodbye my love."

I hung up the phone with probably the worst case of guilt I have ever had. I should never have done what I did but it felt so exhilarating. I was afraid I would have a message from Cade this morning but I had nothing. Maybe I should text him to let him know how much I enjoyed the evening. No, he should contact me. The phone beeped and I grabbed it with excitement only to find a message from Luke saying "It was good to hear your voice this morning. Love you." I texted back "Me too." A little disappointed I put the phone down and decided to take a run. After a quick tooth brushing, I checked my phone again. Still nothing. "That is strange, I know he enjoyed himself every bit as much as I did. Why wouldn't he text me?"

I made coffee and looked out at the work area.

Coming Home

It is coming along very quickly. I am impressed. I do believe that by the end of next week they will be starting the foundation work. I can't believe it's really going to happen. Damn it, why hasn't Cade texted me? Maybe he didn't enjoy the evening like I thought he did. Maybe he thinks I'm nothing but a whore and a cheater! Well the cheater part is right but I am not a whore! Oh Crap! I am going for that run.

I was going to take my phone with me but thought Nope, I'll be just fine without it. Who does he think he is? Just breeze in here with the best sex I have ever had and then not so much as a Hi, how's it going? Oh no, Mr. Tate you have picked the wrong chickie to play this game. I will not be making any phone calls or texts. I'll not play this part. I'll act as those it never happened and move on.

The run was great and the shower afterward was very refreshing. I didn't even look at my phone. I just got dressed and headed to the shop. I was in a mood and things started getting re-arranged. I decided to make some more room for my boots and called John to see about some shelves. He told me to call a guy he knew who did good work and needed the money. I got a hold of him right away and he said he could come down right now. I love it when things come together.

A young man name Jeffrey showed up fifteen minutes later and had some great ideas not only for the boots but also how to add an extra dressing room. I only have two and I hate for people to have to wait forever. He was an amazing young man and was more than willing to get started right away. I gave him some money and sent him to the lumber yard. I was on a roll. The shelves were to be simple but substantial. I went to the computer and started ordering boots. I am going to have so much more room now. It was nearly six when I finally told Jeffrey to stop for the day. He already had one third of the wall done. I didn't want to have to stain anything so we went with redwood and the rustic look is perfect. "What time would you like for me to be here tomorrow Ms. Laurence?" "First of all it's Abby, and how about ten o:clock?" "You got it Ma'am, and thank you." "Actually I should be thanking you. See you tomorrow." "Goodnight Abby." "Goodnight Jeffrey." I thought to myself as he drove away, what a nice young man."

The shop is a complete disaster but once he finishes the shelves everything can go back in place. Tomorrow I think I will move one of my jewelry cases and maybe have Jeffrey install a light in it. Harriet is gonna flip out when she sees what we have done! I straightened a few more things and locked up to go home. It has been a very productive day and I did not look at my phone once!

I couldn't stand it anymore. When I got in the car I grabbed it and checked all my messages. There were none from Cade. Maybe he got the message that I wasn't leaving Luke and gave up on the idea of a relationship that would go nowhere. I was pretty tired from my day's activities and just got a to go meal and

Coming Home

headed home.

I sat on the couch in my sweats and stuffed food in my mouth followed by wine, with the remote control just clicking through channels. During the day I was so busy I didn't have time to think about Cade but now I can't think of anything else. I guess my little speech about Luke must have sunk in and he knows all I will give him is what he got. The only problem is that I really enjoyed what we gave each other. Well I can't risk what I have with Luke for an orgasmic night of sex with Cade.

I was worn out, full, and disgusted. Luke called and he could tell from my voice something was up. "What's wrong babe? You sound agitated." "I'm just tired Luke. I decided to rework the shop today." "What did you do?" "I had a young man start working on some shelves for my boots, and he's also incorporating another dressing room". "Sounds good." The rest of the conversation was pretty much the same as always and I finally said "Goodnight." And went to bed.

The alarm woke me and it dawned on me there was no noise coming from outside! Is it a holiday I don't know about? When I looked out the window I couldn't believe what I saw. The land was all cleared of debris and John was painstakingly working on tearing down the fireplace. I was so wrapped up in everything I hadn't even noticed! I hope to finish the shelves at the shop today because I express shipped my order and the new boots will be here tomorrow around noon. Today I will be clearing a spot for the boxes that the boots come in.

The phone rang and Denny said "Good morning, Abby. I have the final plans ready if you would like to take a look at them and finalize any problems." "That sounds great Denny. Will you be in your office sometime today?" "I'll be here until ten this morning and then back in around three." "I'll swing by on my way to the shop if that will work for you." "I'll see you then." I decided I needed to get going so I got dressed, threw on a little make-up, grabbed my coffee, and set out for Denny's office. I honked and waved at John when I drove by and he smiled and waved back. The plans were perfect except for one little window missing in the bathroom upstairs. "Thank you so much Denny. It's exactly what I was looking for." "You are quite welcome Abby. We will get started as soon as John has leveled everything. The posts will come first for the foundation, the plumbers will come in and put in all the pipes, then we can start the framing and it's all mine, and you can check on productivity everyday." "I'll try not to be a pest!"

I left Denny's and still had time to go by the store and pick up some breakfast tacos to go with our coffee. I noticed yesterday that Jeffrey was drinking coke, so I picked up a six pack for him, and I think we will order from Marco's today. I feel like some good lasagna. Jeffrey was right on time and after saying "Good morning Abby", he went straight to work. He thanked me for the refreshments but said he had a big breakfast at the Wimberley Cafe and maybe he would eat something later. I also told him about the cokes and he seemed pleased. Two hours flew by and it was lunch time. Jeffrey is very good at what he's doing and trying very hard to keep things neat and clean as he works. I have been in the store room moving this and that and feel I will have plenty of room for the boot boxes in an area of bins I had made before I opened. They should fit four to a bin and I have three high and six across. That's a good start. Some I will leave out as a display with the boots. I heard a knock on the back door and Fed Ex was there with my order. "Where would you like them ma'am?" "Just bring them in through here. I signed his form, and he was on his way. I looked at the invoice and noticed there were a few back ordered but they assured me they would arrive within two weeks and with no extra shipping costs to me. I really wanted to jump into them but knew Jeffrey needed some lunch and a break.

    I walked out the storeroom door and could not believe the progress! This boy is a genius. "Jeffrey, you need to slow down. You're gonna hurt yourself!" "I'm fine ma'am." "I am going to Marco's to get us some lunch. What would you like?" "I love their lasagna." "Perfect, me too. I'll be back in a jiff." I walked across the street around the Country diner to Marco's. I gave them my order and got a glass of tea to sip on while I waited. One of the waitress's asked what I was doing working on my day off and I told her about the new edition and all the new boots. "Oh, that sounds fascinating. I'll be over tomorrow on my break to check it out." "Please do, I'd be happy to show them all to you and get some feedback on my choices." I spoke to some of the other locals who were eating, then took my order and went back to the shop.

I nearly had to horse whip Jeffrey to get him to stop long enough to eat. He got a coke from the fridge and asked if I wanted one. I told him I had tea but thank you. We talked during lunch about his family. He has a two year old little girl, and his wife is a secretary for a company in San Marcos. "The construction business is pretty slow right now and I am trying to get as many jobs as I can." "Who keeps your daughter when you are both working?" "My mother-in-law. She's a widow and this is her only grandchild so she takes her every chance she gets. John has promised me some work on your new house." "I am very pleased to hear that. I like your attention to detail. All of these shelves are finished along this wall right?" "Yes ma'am and those on the front wall also. A few more screws and these will be finished too. Then I can work on the dressing room." "So, it will be all right to start putting boots up?" "Yes ma'am, and if you need help with the taller shelves, just let me know." "That's sweet Jeffrey but I'm going to have to be able to get to them when I have customers and you're not here, so I might as well figure that out now."

Jeffrey finished up the dressing room by the end of the day. He integrated corrugated tin in the doors and frames for the mirrors. They went very well with the decor. I might have to change out the other two someday. I told him to come by the shop on Saturday and bring his family. I would love to meet them and I think his wife needs a pair of my boots. He said "Oh no, Abby we couldn't afford these right now." "Who said anything about paying for them?" He grinned and put away his tools. I paid him and he was on his way.

Friday, Saturday, and Sunday proved to be very profitable. I will have to order more boots today. Luke was even excited about the new look and talked me out of a pair of boots! Jeffrey brought his wife by to see his work and I had to force her to pick out a pair. Their little girl is adorable and I got her boot size too. When I get the baby area ready I will order her a pair.

When I arrived home after work I found a box sitting on my porch swing. There was a note from John reading.

I found this behind one of the stones in the fireplace. I thought it might be important.

John

I picked up the box and the memories became so clear once again. We were all sitting around the fireplace with something meaningful in our hands. We were constructing a time capsule. I believe Julie and I were around five at the time. We were suppose to open it when we turned fifty. Under the circumstances, I believe this will be a good year to open it with Tessa on

Darla Hagan

Christmas Eve. It is going to be a hard Christmas without Mom and Dad, maybe these good memories will help the both of us. It was then that I noticed it was locked. How am I going to open it? I remembered the key in the pictures and knew it had to be the one. I will go by the storage building tomorrow and pick it up.

The weather has finally gotten cooler and I have been using the fireplace a lot. There's nothing like a fire to make the stress of the day just drain away. I talked to Tessa and she's coming Christmas Eve., then she will be going to her boyfriends parents for Christmas dinner. I invited him to come with her, not really wanting him to, but he already had plans. I really want to open the time capsule with just the two of us. She's really excited about it. She's coming early and we plan on cooking all day. Then stuff ourselves till we can't move. Luke wanted me to come to his parents but I ask if I could wait until Christmas day. He wasn't happy but after I told him the circumstances he understood and conceded.

Just as planned on Monday I reordered what I needed and took care of receipts and bank deposits. I think I will wait until tomorrow to take it to the bank. I feel a nap coming on! I just snuggled in right on the couch. I looked up to see Cade walking through my door! I dreamily looked at him as he walked to the couch. He got on his knees and we were face to face. I looked into those deep blue pools and couldn't get any words to come out. I just stared as he came closer and when those beautiful sweet lips met mine I was

Coming Home

transformed to another place where everything was perfect and beautiful. He pulled himself up not breaking the kiss and gently lay on top of me holding his body just lightly on mine using those strong tan taunt arms to hold himself. He pulled back to look at me and I put my hands on his face to pull him to me arching my back to meet his touch. The pure sweet pleasure was too much. I had to have more. He raised his head again and smiled that sexy crooked grin. "Abby" I heard knocking and woke from my deep sleep. "Abby, are you there?" Damn, it was a dream. "Coming." I said as I was trying to come out of the fog I was just in. I pulled myself together and got to the door. "Hi Denny. What's up?" "Did I wake you ? I am so sorry. I need for you to come check something out with me if you can." "Sure, let me find my shoes." Crap, I can't even think much less find my shoes! "I'll be right there."

"I wanted to show you an idea I had for an office slash sitting area in your master bedroom" "Okay." He pulled out the plans and laid them on a piece of plywood that was lying on two saw horses. "Since the bedrooms are recessed from the great room I thought we could come out fourteen feet and make another little room with a balcony, all of course with sliding glass doors." "Wow, Denny that is an awesome idea. Let's do it". He grinned and said "Great, I'll get started on the new plans. It won't make any difference with what we have already done for the first floor because we are still working on plumbing. I think you are really going to like this Abby." "I think I am too

Denny. Thanks."

I went back to the cabin and started thinking about Cade again. I really wish Denny had not messed up that dream! Maybe I'll text him. No I can't do that, especially in the state I am in right now! So I called Luke instead. "Hi Babe. To what do I owe the pleasure of this early call?" "I was just sitting here missing you so I thought I'd call and tell you how much." "I miss you too. Terribly so. "How's your day going?" "It's been pretty good but now it's even better. Oh, and Denny came by with a great idea for an office up stairs with wrap around windows." "I am so looking forward to spending Christmas with you and having you all to myself for a whole week." "Me too. Maybe we can do some little mini day trips or something. Is there anything special you would like to do?" "Just being with you is all I want." "Well maybe we can come up with something that involves both." "I'll leave that up to you.". "I better let you get back to work. I love you Luke." "I love you too. Thanks for the call, it really made my day a whole lot better. Bye, Babe." "Bye, my love. See you soon."

The next two weeks flew by and it was everything I could do to keep things ordered and on the shelves. Christmas falls on Wednesday this year so I will have ten days off. I even get to spend New Year's Eve with Luke. I will return on New Year's Day and rest up for the returns and exchange sizes season!

I got the last customer out the door at five after

six! What a day. Thank goodness once again for Cheryl's help. We could not have done it without her. We all sat down and put our feet up. The place was in terrible disarray but it can wait till tomorrow. I got up and pulled two gifts from behind the boot boxes and told the girls how much I appreciated all they have done for me this year. They in turn did the same and we all hugged an laughed. Harriet wanted to come in tomorrow and help me and I absolutely forbade her to do so. "Oh you can be a stubborn child sometimes." "You wouldn't have it any other way." She hugged me and said "Enjoy your Holidays." "You too, and kiss those grand babies for me." Cheryl gave me another hug and we wished each other a Merry Christmas. I jokingly said "I don't want to see either one of you till next year!" I waved goodbye to both and went back to get the cash drawer to put in the safe. I will take care of it tomorrow.

When I came back to turn out the lights and get ready to go I heard a soft knocking on the front store door. I looked up to see Cade standing there with a pitiful look on his face. I went to the door to unlock it. When I opened it he said "I'm really sorry Abby. I know you are closed but I really need to buy a gift for a special person, and knew you would know exactly how to help me. Do you mind working a little overtime?" "Not at all. Come on in Cade." I said as I locked the door behind him. "What did you have in mind?" "I'm not really sure. That's why I wanted your help. We have been seeing each other for about a month and I don't want to do anything that says too much." I felt my heart stop beating when he said seeing someone but kept what I considered a straight face with a smile. "What about a nice scarf? They are all the rage right now, or some kind of jewelry?" "I don't really want to do jewelry but I have seen a lot of women wearing those poofy looking scarves lately. Maybe that would work." "Well, let's see what we have. Do you have a color preference?" He followed me and I could almost taste him. He smelled as wonderful as ever and I could feel his presence behind me. "Here we are." "I'd like something with blue in it. She wears a lot of blue." He picked one up and said "This one looks nice. What do you think?" He was standing so close and held his hat in his hands. The smell of his freshly washed hair mixed with that newly starched shirt and just polished boots was just too much to bear. I had to catch my breath to answer. "I think that is a very nice choice. Would you like for me to gift wrap it for you?" "That would be great but I am already keeping you and I know you have plenty to do." "Nonsense, I can have it wrapped in no time. I'll just be a moment." I walked back to the table we had set up for wrapping. Most things just went in a bag with tissue paper and a ribbon but for special customers and special packages we wrapped them in nice paper. I had almost finished when I heard footsteps behind me. "How have you been Abby?" "Great, Cade. The house is coming along and my daughter is spending Christmas Eve with me. Then I get to spend ten days with Luke. I am looking forward to all of it." I finished tying the ribbon and said "There you go." When I handed the gift to him our hands touched and it was like an electrical shock went through me. I looked up at him and he said "She's a wonderful person and she treats me like a king." I did not know how to react to his statement and just looked into those beautiful blue eyes staring back at me. I took the gift from him and set it on the table. I took him in my arms. I felt such power to his touch. I kissed him long and deep then released him. "I told you once, another place, another time. Let's make that happen Cade. Let's make time just for us maybe once a year." "What are you talking about?" "We have something special, something so strong it has to come out. We should act on that feeling and give in to it even if it only happens once a year!" "Abby, you are not making any sense." My head was spinning from the kiss and what I was saying. I couldn't even make my feet move to send him on his way. His look of bewilderment struck me and I said "Think about it Cade and let me know." I kissed him on the forehead and gave him his package. "It's on the house." He tipped his hat and let himself out.

What the hell just happened? I ran to lock the door and turn out the lights before anyone else decided to come along and turn my world upside down. I ran back to the storage room, sat down, and just shook my head to try and shake out what just took place but all I could do was feel his lips on mine and being in his arms. Did I really just suggest that we have an affair once or twice a year!"

I gathered my thoughts and my things and left

for home. I am still in somewhat of a daze. First of all, he has someone in his life, which should not bother me in the least but I think I actually turned green when he told me. Why does he have this power over me? I know exactly why. I just don't want to admit it. The man is super sexy and awesome in bed that's why! Now to make things worse, he's unavailable. "Damn you Cade Tate, Damn you!"

Coming Home

Chapter 13

I nearly ripped the door off the car getting out, and all but stomped to the cabin. My phone rang and I answered with a stern "What?" "Mom?" "Tessa?" "Mom, are you okay?" "I'm fine dear. I just had some difficult customers today. What's up?" "I was just calling to see if I needed to bring anything for tomorrow." "Tomorrow?" Oh yeah! It's Christmas Eve. "Uh nope. I should have everything we need." "Okay, I will see you around ten." "Looking forward to it. Drive safe." "I will. Love you Mom." "Love you too." Damn you again Cade Tate. Now I have to go back to the store because I have nothing. I just turned around and walked right back out the door.

Darla Hagan

The grocery store was a freaking nightmare. Everyone in town had to have been there. There were screaming children, screaming parents, baskets everywhere, and I needed everything everyone else did. I came really close to just dropping it all and telling Tessa we'd go out to eat! It took about an hour and I was getting down to my last nerve but I made it out with everything. To make things worse I found myself looking at every woman thinking, is that the one he's dating, or maybe that one? That did not help my mood at all!

When I finally made it home and got everything in the house and put away I listened to Luke's message, and fell into bed. I was emotionally drained and exhausted. I am spending a week with the man I love and will have nothing on my mind but my proposal to Cade! I tossed and turned for hours and realized I had not eaten, so I got up and ate some cheese and crackers washed down with a glass of wine. I went back to bed, and set my alarm just in case. I closed my eyes and the alarm went off.

I crawled out of bed and into the shower. I made my bed then started preparations for our dinner. Tessa was right on time. "Hi Mom. The place looks like it is really coming along." "Hi baby, I'm in the kitchen." She came through with packages she put under the tree and went back out to retrieve her traditional pecan pie with chocolate chips in it. "You look beautiful baby girl. What is this blue stuff in your hair?" She laughed. "It's just a few streaks. Don't get all freaky on me." "I'm not. Come here, give me a hug and grab an apron. We have lots to do!"

She poured each of us a glass of wine and began cutting vegetables for the dressing. I had the roasting hen, instead of turkey ready for the oven but it will have to wait till the cornbread is done. We have so much fun talking and laughing in the kitchen this time of year. Just like when she was a little girl. She told me all about her boyfriend and how they were chemistry partners. I think she really likes this one. I've never seen that twinkle in her eyes before. When she talks about him she just lights up. It fills me with so much joy to see her so happy.

"Everything is in the oven. Let's take a glass of wine and go sit on the porch." "I'll get the wine and meet you there." I put on my coat and scarf to ward off the chill and went out to sit on the swing. Tessa wasn't far behind. She handed me the wine and sat down. "Oh Mom, I have such great memories being here with Gran and Pop. I miss them so much." She leaned on my shoulder and I said. "I know sweetie. I do too. We just have to keep these beautiful memories in our minds and hold on to them forever." We just sat and talked until the timer went off on the stove. "Sounds like it's back to work for us."

When the chicken was done I poured the drippings into the dressing and had to add some chicken broth to complete it. I put it in the oven and began the process of preparing the meal for the table. I cut the cranberry sauce, sliced the pies, the rolls were in the oven with the dressing, and had the other sides warming in the toaster oven. Tessa set the table with the good china and silver that I had gotten from the storage building. I began plating everything and she poured the wine and water. We seated ourselves and made a toast to a better year to come. We also said a prayer to Mom and Dad and those who could not be with us.

We ate till I thought I would not be able to move. I put away the food as Tessa put away the dishes. When we finished, it's tradition to take a nap after dinner and open presents later. Tess went to the spare room and I could hear her on the phone before she even got the door closed. I remember being so much in love with Jimmy. I couldn't wait to be with him, especially at Christmas. I went to my room to lie down and decided to call Luke. "Hey babe, Merry Christmas Eve." "Merry Christmas Eve to you. How's Tess." "She's in love. We are suppose to be napping and she hasn't been off her cellphone since she went to the room. It is so good to see her so happy. We are going to open the time capsule which will bring back some very strong memories that will hurt but be good for us at the same time. How's your family? The boys make it okay?" "Yeah, they are all here. I miss you Abby. I can't believe I get a whole week with you!" " I know, I miss you too and am looking very forward to this short vacation and time with you." "Enjoy your Mother daughter time and hurry to me tomorrow." "I will. Goodnight Luke. I will see you soon."

Coming Home

I napped for about thirty minutes, then got up and tried to be quiet as not to disturb Tessa. I got my book and sat on the couch. It wasn't long before she came out and I ask "Did you have a good nap, hon?" "Oh Mom, I didn't sleep. I was too busy talking to Allan" I just smiled and hugged her close. "I love you baby girl." "I love you too Mom. Now let's open gifts!" "Okay!" We started tearing into gifts. None of this save the bow, save the paper crap with us! Tessa has such good taste in gifts and everything she gave me will look so good in my new house. She really seemed to like her boots. I told her we could go to the shop and pick what she wanted but she said "No way. I love these." "I am so glad. I had you in mind when I found them." "Okay mom, it's time to do the capsule. Where is it?" I walked over to the fireplace, removed the box and brought it over and sat down in the floor. The key I had found in the picture box did belong to the time capsule. I took the key and unlocked it. I was just as excited but also sad at the same time. So much has gone on this year, and this is going to throw some of it all back in our face.

I slowly opened the box to find an envelope on top addressed to me. I don't remember putting that there but then I was small and Mom and Dad probably did it later after we put our things in. I laid it aside for later. The first thing I found was a picture of Mom and Dad. It was a much more recent picture than should have been in there. I looked at Tessa and said "They must have cheated. Dad never was very patient when it came to things like this." The next picture was of Julie and me with our dog Sam. "This is Sam our dog. The most beautiful golden retriever, and it was like he knew just what you were saying. He protected Julie and me just like an old Mother Hen with her chicks." I touched Julie's face and a tear fell down my cheek. I pulled out a rabbit's foot and laughed. "Dad gave this to me for luck and I thought he had really killed a rabbit. I cried for days." I pulled out a skate key. "What in the world is that?" Tessa ask. "It's a skate key. When we were little you put your skates on your shoes and this key tightened them so they would stay. I know I am antiquated." "What happened to the skates?" "I'm sure they rusted or got lost along the way." Tessa pulled out a recipe and said "Oh my gosh, it's Gran's special sauce recipe. That was the most awesome sauce in the world!" There was a picture of Julie and I with our first fish we caught off the pier, and Daddy grinning from ear to ear. "This" I said as I pulled out a floppy chewed up doll "was Sam's favorite thing in the whole world." My thoughts went back to Sam lying on the floor between our beds, his doll tucked under his huge paws, keeping a lookout for anything that might bother us. "He was always right there when we went to sleep, and there when we woke up. One morning he didn't get up." "Awe Mom, I bet he was wonderful." I wiped away another tear and took out the next item. It was Dad's favorite fishing lure. "He swore he was going to catch Oog Oog with that one. He was supposedly the largest fish in the river. It never happened." I reached in for the last thing. It was a picture of Mom and Dad on their wedding day. Not a professional one but rather

Coming Home

a candid one that someone took without their knowledge. It looked like they had snuck off for a private moment. They looked so happy and in love, and it showed the time period they lived in so perfectly, from the shoes to the bow tie and the tiny hat Mom wore. Tessa and I just held each other and cried, then sat in silence for a long while. Finally, wiping away tears, Tessa said "We both have to get up early Mom. We should go to bed. Thank you for your beautiful gifts and I love the boots." "Your welcome baby, sleep well." "Good night Mom. I love you."

I put everything back in the box and turned out the light. I walked to my room thinking to myself, how did she grow up so fast? Also thinking how much I truly miss Mom and Dad. With all the wine and the busy day I drifted off quickly. I thought I had just closed my eyes when I heard Tessa whispering "Mom, I am all packed and about to leave." "What? Oh my, I was really sleeping." "Merry Christmas Mom. I love you." "Merry Christmas baby, I love you too and you be very careful." In a flash, she was gone. Oh man, now I have to get myself together and on the road. I grabbed a quick shower, threw on my clothes, put my things in the car along with gifts for Luke's family, poured some coffee in a to go cup and went to leave when I saw the letter from the box. I had completely forgotten about it. I'll just take a minute to read it now. I was about to open the envelope when my cell phone rang. I put the letter down and went hunting for my purse and the phone. "Merry Christmas, babe." "Merry Christmas to you." "Are you on your way?" "I am just walking out the door as we speak." "Well hurry, I can't wait to see you!" "Don't worry, I'm locking the door right now." "See you shortly, and be careful." "I will. Love you and will see you soon." I grabbed my coat and was putting it on and trying to lock the door at the same time. I got in the car, did a mental check list and took off for Temple.

Luke met me at the car. "Oh babe, it's seems like months since I've seen you." "Yeah, well after a week with me, you might be ready for a month away from me." "Never!" He said as he kissed me. "Come on I'll help you with whatever goes in Mom's house. They can't wait to see you." His parents are nice people, his sister, not so much. She's a whiner, and makes everyone else miserable. I just try to stay clear of her. I walked in the door and his Mom gives me a huge hug around all the packages I am carrying. "Abby, It is so good to see you. It has been forever. Here, let me help you with those. Luke tells me good things about your new shop, and I am so sorry about your house and all the problems that have come with it. Have they found out anything yet?" "Not as far as I know. It's a real mystery to everyone involved." "Well we're not going to worry about such things now. It's Christmas and we are to be joyful and thankful for what we do have. "Yes ma'am. Is there anything I can do to help?" "Just sit down and visit and enjoy yourself. How about a glass of wine? I have your favorite." "Absolutely but I can get it. Luke would you like a glass?" "No but I'll take a beer." "Abby." Luke's dad came into the room and gave me a big hug. "It's been way too long since we've seen you, young lady." "I know, it's just hard starting a new business, having your house burn down, finding bodies, blah, blah, blah." "Well I'm glad you are getting away from all that for a few days." "Thank you, I am very happy to be here and you look great. You must be feeling better." "It was either feel better or get thrown out of the house!" We all laughed and Luke's Mom made a cute face at her husband. Then she and I went to the kitchen. I poured myself a glass of wine and got Luke a beer. He and his Dad were sitting in front of the TV watching football of some kind. Luke's sister and her brood had not yet arrived, nor had Luke's children. I went back in the kitchen and sat at the table to talk with his Mom.

    The brood and the kids arrived around the same time. Luke's mom stood up and said "Let the chaos begin." We both giggled and went out to greet everyone. The grandchildren were ready to open presents. The older children had their heads in their I-phones and Luke's sister was already complaining about all the work she had to do to prepare for this day. I offered her a glass of wine but she did not like any we had. She just kissed her Mom on the cheek and flopped in a chair. "I'm exhausted." "Well dear, this should be a pretty relaxing day for you. How about a beer." "That sounds good." Mom got her a beer and she started in on telling us how miserable her life is. I quietly removed myself to the living room. That wasn't much better so I went to the smaller living area with a warm and inviting fire in a small but suitable fireplace. While getting lost in the flames, I suddenly remembered the letter from the box. I went to get my purse and searched through it but no letter. Then I remembered I was about to read it when Luke called and I must have laid it down when I was looking for my phone. Oh well, what's a few more days after all these years. I'm sure they are just telling us how they hope our lives have turned out to be happy and prosperous. I put my purse up and went back to the chair.

Opening gifts was pure hell. Luke's nieces, nephews, great nieces, and great nephews are horrible little creatures! One wanted this, the other wanted that and how come she got more than me! Dinner was even worse. "Lord help me make it through this day, Amen." It seemed like twenty four hours but finally we got out. I thanked everyone and followed Luke to his house. Just the silence of the car was heaven. When we arrived, Luke helped me get everything in complaining that I brought everything I owned! When finished we sat back and listened to the quiet for a long time while watching the twinkling lights on his Christmas tree. It was so nice to be in the arms of the man I love having such a peaceful moment together.

We had decided and agreed not to buy each other anything this year. Our week together would be our Christmas present to each other. I saw a gift wrapped and under the tree and said. "Oh no, Luke, you forgot a gift." He got up and walked over to the tree, picked up the gift, and grinning from ear to ear presented it to me. "Luke, we agreed." "Just open it." I tore into the package and my heart just swelled when I

Coming Home

saw what it was. "Luke where on earth did you find this? It's perfect, and it looks just like it." It was a German made wind up clock like the one my Daddy brought home from the war. It is beautiful wood and the door opens to an ornate face with Roman numerals. It had a pendulum in the back that would move the gears. When it came time to wind it, one of us girls got the honor. "Luke it is beautiful and it will look lovely on my new mantle just like it sat on the old one for so many years." "I'm so glad you like it. I was afraid it would upset you." "No, you could not have given me a better gift. I love you Luke." "I love you Abigail. Just the smile on your face makes this my best Christmas ever."

"Let's get a shower and go to bed. I'm exhausted." "Together?" "Sure, why not. I'll grab the towels, you get the water ready." I jumped up and ran past him and he chased me touching and kissing along the way. I started the water and started to strip. He gathered what we needed and we both climbed in laughing and fondling each other. "Come on now Luke, I'm tired. Let's get this done and go to bed. Turn around and I will do your back." Reluctantly, he turned around. I soaped him from top to bottom and then rinsed him. "Now turn." "All right." I started very slowly soaping his shoulders, his chest, went around the special part and soaped his legs. On my way back up I took his hardness in my soapy hands and heard a low moan as he put his hands in my hair. I let the water run over him before taking him into my mouth. He had to hold on as his knees went weak. "Oh babe, that's feeling mighty good." "You sound like you're in pain. Do you want me to stop?" "No." He said as I took him in deeper. "Ahhh, babe if you keep this up, then I am not going to make it out of this shower." "Shhh, just relax and enjoy." He leaned back against the wall of the shower and tried several times to stop me but I was on a mission and there was no way I was going to quit till I was ready. He came hard and quick. I used my hand to finish him because I don't swallow! "Good thing we are in the shower or we would have quite the mess to clean up." I came up on my feet and put my wet body against his and gave him a very long sensual kiss, then I looked at him and said "Now you have to wash my hair!" "Oh Lord, you're gonna have to give me a minute to get my eyesight back!" I laughed and switched places with him in the shower. He got the shampoo and started washing and caressing my head and hair. "This shampoo smells so good." "It's the same thing I always use. You're just still in your Aura and things are more intense." "Have I told you Abigail Laurance that I love you?" "Why, yes you have. Turn around and rinse." I told him to go ahead and I would finish. It would be a shame to waste that good feeling by having to wash my hair. He agreed and got out. I finished the shower, dried my hair, brushed my teeth, and put on my jammies. When I got to the bedroom, Luke was already lightly snoring. "Yes." I said with a quiet fist pump. All I want to do is sleep. Mission accomplished!

I awoke to the smell of coffee and bacon. The sun was peeking through the curtains. I stretched and

Coming Home

made myself get up. I would much rather lie here all snuggly but Luke has gone to all of the trouble to fix breakfast. The least I could do is show up. I made my way to the bathroom and halfway made myself look presentable and brushed my teeth. Walking to the kitchen I heard voices. I stopped since all I had on was shorty pajamas. I listened for a minute and could tell it was Luke's Mom. I didn't want to eavesdrop so I started back to the bedroom when I hear her say. "All I'm saying Luke is you're not getting any younger and the business can practically run itself. You need to take the next step with Abby." What? No Abby is not ready for the next step. Tell her Luke. Abby is not ready! "Mom, we've been through this. Abby just started her business. She loves what she does and I'm not going to take that away from her." "Good job, Luke." I whispered to myself. "What are you going to do if she finds someone else? She's a beautiful, wealthy, unattached woman Luke. I'm sure there are plenty of men out there that would scoop her up in a minute." "I just have to trust that she loves me enough to not let that happen." "I don't understand these long distance relationships. In my day It was said absence makes the heart grow fonder... for someone else!" "Think about it Mom. What would I do all day while she's working? I would go nuts." "She can hire someone just like you would to run the business." "No, I am not going over this again. The time is not right. When it is time, you will be the second one to know. Now scoot while I spend the day with my girl." "Okay but remember what I said and don't make me have to say I told you so." "Bye Mom." I ran back to the bathroom and splashed water on my face to make it look like I was just finishing up. Luke came up behind me when I had the towel on my face and I nearly jumped out of my skin. He started laughing and I punched him playfully in the belly "You scared the wits out of me. You can't just sneak up on someone like that." He held me in his arms and said "You mean like you just did." "What?" "Babe, I saw you in the mirror." I started to protest but knew it would never work, so we both just laughed. "That's just mean." "Did I answer correctly?" I didn't answer and he kissed me with a grin and said "Let's eat."

I had done a little research about Waco and thought we might visit the Texas Rangers Museum. I love Texas history and I don't know much about the Rangers. There is also a suspension bridge that was the longest in the world when it was built, and the only bridge across the Brazos. And then there's the Dr. Pepper building where it all started. I really don't care what we do, I just want to be away. Luke surprised me with a rented cabin on Lake Whitney for three nights. Luke, me, the water, and no people. Sounds like a very good plan to me.

Today I just want to chill out all day. I don't even want of get out of my pajamas. We cleaned the kitchen and took our coffee to the living room. "I had pulled up information on some places I thought we might visit." I was trying to show him the print outs I had done but he wasn't even listening to me. He was into something on the computer. I just put them down and picked up my phone. "How's my proposition sounding today?" I texted to Cade. I didn't expect a response but was just in the mood to be devious.

I went to the bedroom to unpack and repack for our three day trip to the cabin. Luke, I found out by getting in his face, is working on a huge deal that would bring a lot of revenue to his company and it is looking like a working vacation. Luke peeked in and said "I missed you. What are you doing?" "I'm putting my things away and packing for the lake." He came over and hugged me and apologized for having his head in the computer. "It's okay baby, I know how important this is to you." "None of it means as much as you do. What would you like to do today?" "I really just want to relax and enjoy the quiet in the arms of the man I love." Let's talk Luke. I mean really talk. We have been together for a while now and we don't really know a lot about each other. I mean things we did when we were younger, our past marriages. We only tell each other the bad side of things. Let's find some positives in our past." He gave me that oh shit the let's talk look that every man gives a woman when he hears that. When he moaned I pushed him away and said "Oh never mind." He grabbed me and threw me on the bed. "I'll talk to you all day Abigail." I smiled and brushed his hair out of his eyes and kissed him. "Thank you." "Now, what would you like to tell me?" "I've really been missing Julie, and Mom and Dad. I suppose it has something to do with this time of year. She didn't even call or send a gift to Tess which is unusual. Not the call, cause she never called me, just Mom and Dad but she always sent something for Tessa." "What really happened between you two?" "Just as I have told you before. She hated Jimmy and when we were dating she would disappear anytime he came over. It was around that time that she switched majors and decided to join the designing world. When Jimmy and I got married I wanted her to be my maid of honor. She wouldn't even come to the wedding." "What did Jimmy think about all that?" "Looking back, Jimmy only cared about Jimmy. When I got pregnant he went ballistic." "You are having an abortion, right?" "When I told him she was a symbol of our love and no way was I going to throw that down some dumpster like yesterdays newspaper. He actually left me for a week but came back begging for forgiveness and talking to my belly saying." "I'm so sorry little one." "When she was born he was off at some convention and when I called he really wasn't jumping for joy. He just said." "Good Job. I'll be home day after tomorrow." "I knew by then I had made a grave mistake by marrying him but I hoped Tessa would make a difference. It didn't. He was gone more and more and rather than fight I just gave in and told him I wanted a divorce. The rest is history. Your turn."

"Leslie and I met in college also. She was sort of a free spirit but I really liked that about her. We dated for two months before we moved in together. A month after we moved in we found out she was pregnant. I've never told anyone this but I'm not completely sure Thomas is biologically mine." "Luke,

Coming Home

really? You've never made any indication that you felt that way." "As far as I'm concerned he's mine. Always has been and always will be. She worked as an archeology professor at Baylor. She enjoyed her job. Sometimes I think more than she enjoyed us. Then we had Joseph and she started becoming distant. I thought it was because of the post postpartum thing but it continued for years. When the boys were old enough to pretty much be left on their own until I got home from work she started making trips overseas. She was living in tents and doing more and more digs. She also turned to food to feed her need for whatever she thought she was missing. The boys grew distant from her and finally I just said fuck it and filed for divorce. It was no surprise but she wanted her, as she called it, fair share. You know all about that so we won't go into it. What about Tessa's boyfriend?" "Well apparently they have been an item for several months. I have yet to meet him and this weekend is her first time to meet his parents. I think she might be in love."

The phone rang and Luke said "Sorry babe, I have to take this." He kissed my cheek and went out the door. I'm so glad I brought my Kindle so I will have something to do! My phone beeped and there was a message from Cade. I felt a tingle in my tummy and swiped to read it. "I just had a most wonderful Christmas and thinking about anything other than that is out of the question right now." "Well that's not a no!" Luke walked back in just as I was settling in to read. "Hey Abigail, how about dinner at Milliliters tonight?" Normally I would jump at that offer but not tonight.

Darla Hagan

"Luke if it is all the same to you I'd rather just stay in. I'll make spaghetti and garlic bread." "Well, I really need to meet this client and I thought it would be a good time." "Damn it Luke I don't feel like entertaining your clients. Why didn't you just tell me instead of trying to trick me into something?" "I wasn't going to trick you into anything. I was going to tell you. I just thought it would be better if you really wanted to go." "Well, no. I don't want to go but you feel free to do whatever. I'm sorry Luke. I know this is important but I came here to relax and be with you. I will be fine tonight by myself but if you plan on working all week, we will have to do this another time."

I went back to reading my book and Luke shook his head and walked out of the room. I spent most of the day reading. I did get up and eat something. I don't know where Luke was, probably working on something in his office. I took a nap after I ate and he woke me when he came in to take a shower and get ready to go. I didn't move. I just pretended I was sleeping. When he came out of the shower I sat up in bed and said,"Good luck tonight, I love you." His eyes softened when I said that and he came over and held me. "I'm truly sorry babe. It's just bad timing. I promise after tonight I will be all yours." We kissed a long slow kiss and I smiled at him. "Go get em Tiger." He laughed, finished getting dressed and said "I'll be back soon. I love you Abigail Laurence." "I love you too."

Luke was true to his word for the three nights at the cabin but had to get back to work on Monday. I

Coming Home

decided to go home. I want to make sure everything is right for Thursday at the shop. I probably will cut back a little on inventory now that Christmas is over. Then pick back up around the time for Spring break. Luke wasn't happy that I was leaving but I could not see sitting around his house all day when I could be at my own being constructive. I have decorations to take down and put back into storage. I need to wash sheets and just give the cabin a general dusting and scrubbing. He pouted but finally came around to the idea.

We said goodbye early Monday morning and I promised to text when I got home. It really turned out to be a sucky vacation and now I have nowhere to be for New Year's Eve! The drive home was miserable as it usually was on I-35. Thank goodness for the new toll roads that get me around Austin. It is a little out of the way but so much less stressful. The town was pretty quite as most of the shops were closed for the holidays. I stopped at the grocery store and picked up some basics. I had plated and frozen several dinners from the Christmas Eve left overs. I love left over Thanksgiving and Christmas dinner!

Darla Hagan

Chapter 14

No work had been done on the house since I left so everything looked pretty much the same. I might take a walk through the house later after everything is put away. I managed to get it all in even though some of it would be going to storage until the house was finished, Maybe I can take all that tomorrow. With sheets in the washer and clothes put away I sat down on the couch for a short rest. At least until the washer buzzed and I had to move one load to the dryer and load another in the washer. I noticed the letter from the box and decided it would be a good time to read it. I know it is going to make me cry and I have been putting it off.

Coming Home

I opened it and laid back on the couch to find out what Mom and Dad had to say:

My Dearest Abigail,

It is with a heavy heart to be writing these words to you. First and foremost we want you to know we love you very much and you have brought more joy and happiness to our lives than we ever thought possible.

Your Mother and I have spent many hours contemplating how to say this to you. It breaks my heart that you have to know what I am about to tell you.

Much to our surprise we had a knock on the door only to find Jimmy and Julie standing there. We did not know what to think about it. We were so excited to see Julie but confused as to why she was with Jimmy.

Darla Hagan

They sat down and Julie started crying and telling the story that will unfold before us. It all started when y'all were in college. When you were dating Jimmy, Julie was secretly seeing him. Julie did not want to hurt you and moved to California so she could put distant between them. She also knew he would have business trips and they could meet and you would be none the wiser.

They were about to tell you everything the same day you had the news that you were pregnant and Julie was not happy about this. She told Jimmy she would not see him anymore if he did not marry you. Your Mother and I were furious for what the two of them put you and Tessa through. I got up and tried to work things out in my head when Jimmy came up behind me and put his hand on my shoulder. He began to tell me he never really meant to hurt you but he loved Julie. I did not want him to touch me. I had such rage at the time and when he said he really wasn't ready for a child either but wanted to do the right thing. It was just all building up inside me and when I turned around to confront him, I shoved him with all my strength. I guess I just could not stand the thought that they could put you and Tessa through something that horrid.

He fell back and hit his head on the edge of the fireplace. I thought I had knocked him out and that made me feel better but that was not the fact. Julie started slapping his face and trying to wake him but there was a lot of blood and we finally realized, he was not going to get up. I had killed him. Abby, I swear this was never my intention.

Darla Hagan

We all panicked and finally decided to bury him beneath the slab in the sun room. They were to pour the concrete in the morning, so we waited until dark and removed some of the concrete wire and dug out a grave. We wrapped him in garbage bags and put him in the hole, covered it up and replaced the wire. We hoped and prayed they would not notice.

I know what we did was wrong but I just couldn't bring anymore hurt to you and Tess.

They poured the slab the next day without any problems and we knew we were in the clear. No one knew Julie was here and we sent her home that same night after we all got Jimmy buried.

The only way this will ever be found out is when you do the time capsule and

Coming Home

that is why I put the letter in with it. I wanted you and Tessa to have the best life you could without having to know the truth.

If you have opened this when you were suppose too, you should be 60 by now and have beautiful grandchildren with the memories of Jimmy long gone.

Forgive us my child but every time we walked into that room, or saw you or Tess, it was a reminder of what we had done. Jimmy deserved what he got but Mom and I could not bear the horrible things we had done.

This is Goodbye my darling child. Please try and find it in your heart to forgive us. We could not forgive ourselves. We both love you so much and know that you and Tessa have grown into strong *beautiful women.*

Love you forever

Mom and Dad

I looked at the letter in disbelief for what seemed hours. Why would Julie do such a thing? Why didn't they call the police and tell them it was an accident? Why, why, why? Oh my God, they didn't swerve off the road to miss a deer. They ran off the road on purpose! The tears hit hard. I was throwing things and screaming at God. I wanted Jimmy to be alive so I could kill him myself. As for Julie, she is dead to me, and she will pay for her part in all of this. I will take this letter to Dean and they can bring her back her for trial. How am I gonna tell Tessa? How am I going to tell anyone?

This explains why Julie left, and why she never talked with us. It explains why Jimmy was always in such a good mood when he had to go on business trips. It explains why he grew to hate me so much as our marriage progressed. It was because he was in love with Julie and I trapped him with a baby he did not want.

I held the letter and curled up into a ball on the couch. I held my knees with my arms, cried, and rocked for hours. This was all Jimmy's fault. Why did he have to come into our lives? I actually loved him,

Coming Home

and the whole thing was just a farce. He didn't want me. He wanted her! I couldn't even say her name. How could she do this to me, to all of us? If I had not become pregnant, things would have been different. I could tell in the weeks after I told him I was pregnant that there was a change in Jimmy but just put it off to wedding and baby jitters. If I had not become pregnant, there would not have been a wedding. At least not one between me and Jimmy. I am such a fool.

No! They are the fools. Look what they have done. Selfish, greedy, dishonest, self serving... I can't even stand to think about it. Julie! Not only did she take my daughter's father, my husband but she killed our parents! "I hate you Julie, I hate you!" I screamed and beat on the pillow until I was in a rage of tears and sweat. I got up and stomped into the kitchen for a glass of water. I couldn't breathe. I couldn't think. I took a drink of water and walked the floor trying to catch my breath. I heard something in the other room and felt strong hands on my shoulders. I was still breathing very short breaths and had a rage in my eyes when I turned to see Cade standing over me. "Abby? Are you okay? What happened?" "Cade, I can't breath." He sat me in a chair and put my head between my legs and rubbed my back, chanting, "breath, relax, breath." After a few moments I gained a little control and jumped into his arms. "Abby, tell me what's wrong." I couldn't talk I was still sobbing so hard. He pushed me back by my shoulders and shook me. "Abby. What is going on? Did someone hurt you? Did someone break in? Tell me. What is going on?"

Darla Hagan

I caught my breath and looked blankly for a moment, then I moved away to look for where I had thrown the letter. When I saw what I had done to my living room, I understood why he was so concerned. I was blindly looking under pillows, magazines, and papers. "What are you looking for?" "The letter. I've got to find the letter. It's evidence." I was throwing things and looking under everything. "Evidence? Evidence for what?" I must have had a wild look in my eyes because he took me by the shoulders again and said "Abby. You are not making any sense. I can't help you if you don't tell me what the hells going on! What letter?" Just then, I saw it. I jerked away from him and grabbed it. "This letter. This letter, that's made my whole life a lie. This letter that's torn my world into a million little pieces. This letter!"

He sat me down on the couch and took the letter. He sat beside me and started to read. I couldn't even look at him, I just sat and rocked back and forth. I shuddered when he finished and lay the letter on the coffee table. He leaned back on the couch and pulled me close and held me. He stroked my hair and soothed me with his soft whispers. He felt so good and the compassion he was giving was just what I needed. I finally stopped crying and my breathing became normal again. I relaxed against him and fell asleep.

I awoke sometime during the night sill in Cade's arms. He had not moved the entire time. When I stirred he softly said "I think you should lie down for a while. I will stay with you if you want." "I would like that very much." He helped me to my room and removed my shoes. He undid my blouse and took it off. Then looked around for something to put on me and found a big T-shirt. He carefully removed my bra and slipped the shirt over my head. He then removed my pants, and lay me back on the pillows, and covered me with the quilt. I heard him moving something and opened my eyes to see he had removed his boots and was siting in a chair with his feet propped on the bed. "Cade?" "Yes." "Would you mind lying with me? You don't have to get under the covers, just be close enough to touch." He did not say a word, just came around to the other side of the bed and held my hand. This simple gesture made me feel so calm that I drifted off to sleep.

I woke up screaming and strong arms were there to hold and soothe me. "I was dreaming. I could see my Mom and Dad holding hands and swerving off the road. It was horrible?" I was shaking and Cade said "It was just a dream, Abby. Try to go back to sleep." "But it's not just a dream, Cade. It is completely real. My parents are gone and it's my fault." "How is it your fault. Listen to me Abby. Your parents chose their own destiny. The facts leading up to that matter are clear. None of this is in any way your fault." He lay me back down and held me close and stroked my head till I was once again asleep.

Cade had put a blanket across the window to keep it as dark as he could. He knew she needed to rest before confronting all this again. It had been a fitful night for both of them and he was awakened again by a moan and hearing "Go away. You're the reason for all of this." She was hitting at the air with her fist and Cade grabbed them once more and soothed her back to sleep.

It was after two before she finally woke up. Cade had been up but close by. He had made coffee and found some pastries in the freezer. He had just finish downing a cup when she opened her eyes and looked at him. "Cade. You're still here? That means" She trailed off. "It wasn't just a bad dream. It is real" "Yes Abby. I'm, afraid it is very real, and we need to get some food into you and get you out of this bed." I looked around and ask. "How did I get here, and why are you here?" "I was driving by and saw you were back so I was going to talk to you about some things and heard screaming and the sound of things being thrown so I let myself in after you didn't answer. I thought someone was in your house and you were fighting them off." "There was someone in my house. Demons from my past." "I know, you showed me the letter. You had a very bad night. You kept waking up screaming or talking, and I could not bring myself to leave you that way."

I got up and went into the bathroom and closed the door. I looked in the mirror and saw a stranger looking back at me. Someone who had been living a lie for all these years. Someone who was foolish enough to believe her husband truly loved her. "He never loved you." I said to the mirror. "He only loved himself and

Coming Home

your sister!" My sister, I can't even begin to imagine how they could do this to me, to Tessa! It certainly explains the absent of both of them. "Oh my God how am I going to tell Tess all of this? Should I contact the police, or should I tell her first. Should I try to reach Julie or let the police do it? It's all too much. My head is swimming.

I washed my face and tried to make something of my hair. My eyes were swollen and I looked and felt like hell but I didn't care. I walked into the kitchen and Cade was making me a sandwich. "Cade. Thank you for doing all this but I don't think I can eat anything right now." "You can and you will. Now come over here and sit." I slowly walked to the chair and noticed what a mess I had made out of the living room. He ask me "Mayo or mustard?" "What? Oh mayo." He finished the sandwich and poured a glass of milk. He sat both in front of me and I felt nauseous. "Abby, you've got to eat. Now pick up the sandwich and take a bite." The last thing on my mind was food but Cade was right. I couldn't function without something in my system.

I ate half of the sandwich and drank all the milk. "Very good, now what can I do to help you through this" "You've done quite enough Cade. Thank you for being here and watching over me, but I think I need to work this out myself." "I am not leaving you till I know at least someone is on their way to be with you." "I think the first thing you should do is get a shower. It might make you feel better, then we can call the sheriff." "Oh Cade, I don't know if I am ready for that yet." "Do you have a way to reach your sister?" "Just a cell phone number she never answers." "If she knows your calling for this she probably will not return your call. She may even leave the country. If she hasn't already. Do you have an address, a state, anything?" "Nothing but that cell phone number." "When the sheriff finds out that this case is solved, someone will have to claim the body." "Let the state have him. They can bury him in a pine box in a shallow grave for all I care." "I don't think that's gonna happen but does he have any family that you know of." "No, he was an orphan and worked himself up the real estate ladder. I don't even know where he lived. I just know the checks for Tessa came every month through the court. Even when he sent extra money, he did it through the court."

"I think we are going to have to make an excuse to get her back here. One that is strong enough to make her come. Do you have any ideas?" "Cade, right now I can't even think straight."

Cade told me to go and take my shower and he would clean up the dishes. I climbed in the shower and fell apart. I started crying again and letting the water wash away the tears. I just can't believe all that has happened. I feel like I have lost everything that ever meant anything to me, because my sister was in love with my husband. Why didn't they just tell me in the beginning, none of this would have happened. On the other hand I guess when I got pregnant with Tessa he felt an obligation to me. Or Julie felt an obligation and made him do the right thing and marry me. Tessa is the one thing I would not change in all of this. She is my world.

I let the water run over me hoping to wash away all that happened. When I finished, nothing felt better, nothing changed. It still hurt like hell. Cade knocked on the door to make sure I was okay and I replied "I'm fine. I'll be out in a minute." I just needed one more minute to pull myself together. I need to call Tessa and Luke, and oh yeah, come up with an idea of how to get Julie here or at least get an address so the police can find her. Maybe Dean can help us with that.

I went out and Cade had cleaned up the living room. He said "I'm sorry but I'm not sure I put things where they should be." "Everything looks great. Thank you so much for everything." He took me by the shoulders and said "You are a lady with troubles and in need of a friend. A true gentleman would never leave a lady in distress. My Grandmother would turn over in her grave." I smiled and said "Thank you so much. I am going to call Luke and Tessa. I think you have gone above and beyond. You don't have to stay." "I would like to stay until I know Luke is close. I really don't want to leave you alone." "That's very sweet but what about work?" "It's the Holidays. I am off for the next few days." "What about your girlfriend?" We have a very open understanding about our relationship. She doesn't ask and neither do I."

Darla Hagan

My phone rang and I let the machine pick up. "Hi babe. I'm sorry I didn't call last night but I finalized the deal. It's going to be a real boost to the firm's economy. I'd like to come see you if you're not too mad at me. I love you. Call me when you can. I can be on the road anytime." I listened as he talked and the joy in his voice made me mad. "How dare he be so happy when I am so miserable?" "He doesn't know you're miserable, remember?" "I know I'm being ridiculous and selfish. That big high he's on right now is about to be shot to Hell!" I picked up the phone to call and tell him I need him as soon as he could get here. "I'm on my way." I turned around and Cade had gone out on the porch to give me some privacy. I called Tessa and asked her to come as soon as she could that I had something that couldn't wait. She wasn't happy but said she would be here as soon as she could. I walked out on the porch with Cade and said "I'll never be able to thank you enough for taking care of me through this." "Think nothing of it Abby. I would have done it for anyone. It's just what you do when friends are in need." I smiled and looked out over the river as he got a blanket and wrapped it around me.

"How long do you think it will be before they get here?" "I asked Tessa to text me when she was leaving San Marcos, and Luke to text me when he got to San Marcos." "This is a very serious situation Abby and the police are going to have a lot of questions. I know this is a bad way to do this but would a major trauma in Tessa's life bring Julie home?" "No, I would never use my daughter for something like that! I don't know if she would come for me but I would rather it be me than Tessa. She's been through enough." "That sounds like a good plan, and remember Julie has been through all these losses too. She has to have some remorse." "I doubt that, given her part in this and no communication about it." "Y'all can get together and toss around ideas before you call the Sheriff. They can apprehend her at the airport." "I'm not good at lying. I don't know what to do." "Don't worry about it the Sheriff will help you and your family." "Oh Cade, I don't know how I would have gotten through last night without you." I held him very close for a few minutes and he rubbed my back with pure compassion. "By the way. Why were you here last night?" "We can talk about that later. You just try to stay calm till everyone gets here." Cade left when Luke texted me from San Marcos. He hugged me and kissed my forehead. "Everything will be okay." He turned to walk away and I felt a piece of my heart go with him.

Darla Hagan

Chapter 15

When Luke arrived, Tessa pulled in right behind him. They both all but ran to me and I broke down as she hugged me and said "Mom. What is it. You're scaring me." Luke stood close and took my hand. I pulled back and said "Come on inside. I have something to show you both." They followed me in the house and sat on the couch. I gave Tessa the letter first. Luke sat beside me and held my hand with a perplexed look on his face. He brushed my hair back from my wet face and gently kissed my forehead. It was the same gesture Cade had just done and I felt a pang of guilt run through me. "What?" Tessa screamed. "Mom. Does this mean what I think it means?" She handed the letter to Luke and I took her in my arms and we rocked back and forth. "Yes, baby. I'm afraid it does." She jumped out of my arms and said "But how could they do that to us? It was Dad, it's always Dad. Why did you marry him, why did..." she broke into sobs. Luke had finished the letter and took her over to the couch and sat her down. He put his arm around her and was trying to soothe things for her. "It was an accident. A very unfortunate accident." She stood up again and screamed "Not Gran and Pop. That was no accident. That was Dad! I hate him . I hate that I have his blood running through my veins. I just want to kill him with my bare hands. Oh yeah, I can't cause Pop already took care of that." She sat back down crying again. I put my arms around her again and said "Let it all out baby. I did the same thing last night." She just sat between us and cried and cried.

    Luke made some sandwiches and made Tessa and, myself sit down at the kitchen table and eat. I didn't realize how hungry I was and that half a sandwich was long gone. I used quite a bit of energy the past 18 hours or so. Tessa just picked at hers, and the look on her face just crushed my heart. She stopped and said "I'm going home. I need time to process all this" "Honey are you sure you want to do this?" "Yes, I want to be alone for a while to try and come to terms with this." "Okay, please be careful and call me if you need anything." "I will Mom." With a kiss on the cheek and an I love you, she was gone.

    I turned from the door and Luke was there, arms

open and a smile on his face. "Come here baby. Let me hold you for a while." "I fell into his arms and went limp. The past hours had really taken a toll on my body, mind, and soul. "We need to talk about how to bring Julie to justice." "Can we just sit, hold each other, and not think about anything for a while?" "Absolutely."

We sat in silence for a long time, at least I did. Luke could not be still if his life depended on it. If there was a game on, it would be another story. I started thinking how sweet Cade had been and Luke paled in that department, not that he wasn't a gentleman, he just wasn't a patient gentleman. They are as different in some ways as night and day. Together they make the perfect man. Where Cade is gentle and knows the right things to whisper softly in my ear, Luke is at a loss for words.

Luke came in from the kitchen with a cup of hot tea. "I made you a cup of tea." I hate hot tea. He should know that but I took it and said "Thank You." He ask me when I wanted to talk to the sheriff and I said "Please not today. You can call and ask him to come out tomorrow." Luke got his phone and looked up the number. He waited a few minutes and said "Sheriff I don't know if you remember me but I am Abby Laurence's friend, Luke Robinson." The sheriff must have said yes, because Luke began talking. "Sheriff we have some new evidence in the Jimmy Laurence case we would like to share with you." He listened and then said "No sir, tomorrow would be better for us. How about eleven or so? That sounds great sir. Thank you and we will see you tomorrow." Luke hung up and said he had something at eleven but could come around one. I curled into a ball and said "Okay." Luke told me it would be better after it gets done. "Hopefully he will have some way or ideas as to how to get Julie back down here." "Yeah, maybe" I said half halfheartedly. "I really just don't want to talk about it anymore right now." "Would you like to watch a movie? I could go get something." "That might be a good idea. We can pop some corn and have a coke." "Movie, popcorn, and coke coming up." He said as he kissed the top of my head. "I'll be back in a flash!"

I could really care less about a movie but maybe he will bring something that will take my mind off things. I had a huge sudden craving for a glass of milk. I got up and poured out the tea and replaced it with milk and a couple of ice cubes. I looked in the cabinet for the pecan sandies and got two to dunk in my milk. There's just something about ice cold milk that makes you feel good all over. I got my pillow from the bed, and a blanket. I put some more wood in the fireplace and settled in on the couch.

I finished the cookies and milk, put away the evidence, and settled back in on the couch. I turned on the the TV and channel surfed for a while then turned it off. When I lay the remote back on the table I noticed the letter and that lonely feeling in the pit of my stomach returned. Thank goodness Luke came back quickly. He said "I couldn't find anything new and I know you've seen RV but I also know you really like it, so that's what I got. If that doesn't do it. I will sit through four hours of Gone with the Wind with you!" "I love RV and I may take you up on the other. We'll see. You go pop the corn and I'll get the movie ready." "It's a deal." He handed me the movie and kissed me before he went to pop the popcorn.

Somewhere between Robin Williams character getting the RV stuck on the hill and when it hit the water I fell sound asleep. I woke up in the morning still on the couch, still in my clothes and thought back to the night before when Cade so carefully undressed me and put me to bed, then lay beside me. Luke was no where in sight! I did smell coffee and rose from my so called bed to get some. I looked out the front window and saw Luke on the pier fishing. So much for compassion and comfort!

I checked the clock and had plenty of time for a shower before Dean should arrive. The light on my cell was blinking and I checked to see if it was Tessa. It was from Cade. "Are you doing okay?" I was again overcome with emotion at how much he cared. I looked out the window at Luke and texted back. "I'm fine. Thank you so much for all you have done." "You are quite welcome and let me know if there is anything else I can do." "I will." I left it at that and took my shower.

Dean arrived promptly at one. I ask him in and if he would like something to drink. "No ma'am I'm just fine, Thank you. Now what is this new evidence you have on the Laurence case?" I explained the box in the fireplace and how we came to find the letter, then handed it to him to read.

When he finished he looked at me and said "I'm sorry for your losses, Abby. I know this must have hit you hard." A tear rolled down my cheek as I said "Yes, it has." "Now, I do have one problem. Your sister is an accomplice in covering up an accidental homicide." I shook my head and said "Yes, I understand." "Do you have an address so I can have her picked up and bring her back here for trial?" "No, I don't. I have a cell phone number and that is all. As far as I know she doesn't even know the house is gone!" We looked up and Tessa was standing in the kitchen door way. She had come in through the back door. "I know how to reach her." She looked at me and said "I'm sorry Mom but Julie and I talk about once a month. I don't know where she is or what she does but we do keep in touch." "Tessa you don't have to apologize to me for talking to your Aunt." "Do you think you can get her to come see you?" Asked the sheriff. "I don't know. I've never ask that of her before." "Maybe we can use the phone number to track her down. These new computers have all kinds of information on them. Let me get that number and run it through the system. I'll have to keep the letter also." "I understand." "Okay, I'll take this to the office and see what I can find out. I will get back to you as soon as I know anything." He hugged me and said his condolences again, then tipped his hat before he walked out the door.

Darla Hagan

Tessa was in my arms seconds later crying. "It's okay baby." "No it's not Mom. I should have known this. My whole life has been one great big farce." "Now you look at me. I feel we had a pretty great life." "I didn't mean it that way." "I know. I honestly do." Luke jumped in and said "Let's go eat somewhere. We need to get out of here for a while." "I think that is a great idea but let's go to Dripping instead of here." "Sounds good to me. Mom I'm sorry." "Stop saying that, This is not your fault. Come on let's go to Thyme and Dough." "Oh I haven't been there in ages. I am so ready." "Nothing like fresh baked goodies to soothe the soul!"

The ride to Dripping Springs was quiet but comfortable. We saw several young bucks playing in a field and some lazy does with their yearlings lying at the edge of the trees. The restaurant closes at three and we arrived at two thirty. It was crowded as usual but we found a table easily. I got the chicken salad and Tessa and Luke had turkey sandwiches. They were all yummy and the little extras like fresh berries in your flavored tea or water just made it so pleasant. We left with Italian Cream Cake, Carrot Cake, and German Chocolate cake for later.

We decided on the way home to stop at the store and get a few things. I'm sure after such a good meal this late in the day we will not be hungry for a while. Some small snack and our desserts will be perfect for later. We talked Tessa into staying the night and watched a movie. Snacks and dessert came after the

Coming Home

movie and then off to bed.

My sleep was restless and the morning came with no relief. Nothing had changed except I had my loving boyfriend and my beautiful daughter here to share in the pain. It is so nice to have both of them here and when I did crawl out of bed, Tessa and Luke were in the kitchen cooking breakfast. I stood at the doorway watching as Tessa flicked a spoonful of pancake mix right into Luke's face. He returned the favor by breaking an egg over her head. I saw the look on Tessa's face and I knew what was about to happen, so I came in to stop the madness. They looked at each other, smiled and hit me with pancake mix and an egg. "Oh, you are on guys" I said as I gather mix into both hands and rubbed their faces with it. We had a free for all and made a huge mess but laughed our asses off. It was just what we needed for some release.

Needless to say breakfast clean up took a while but we all felt better. I really need to go to the shop just to check on things. Tessa finally agreed to come with me. She always knows she will find something she likes and I will give it to her. I keep trying to tell her that's what a Mother is for but she's so damned independent it's ridiculous.

The shop was fine and Tessa came away with a pair of booties, not the baby kind but western shoes that look like boots. I'm told they made them years ago for the country stars because under pants you couldn't tell they were not boots and they were so much cooler for the performers under all the bright lights and hot outdoor shows. She got an adorable red pair and a blouse to set them off. That was all I could talk her into and I had to almost break something to get her to take them.

What a great way to start off a new year! At least we can keep this under wraps for a while. It will all come out if they ever find Julie and there is a trial. I went to the shop to prepare it for returns on Thursday and Luke went home. I didn't even make black eyed peas and cornbread. I figured what's the use. Eating some stupid peas is not going to change my luck!

The phone rang and it was Dean. He had Tessa call Julie and when she called back, they traced her to none other than New York! They are getting in touch with the New York Police Department in hopes of picking her up. If they find her and have her in custody, then one of the police officers from here will fly there and escort her back to Hays County.

Just as suspected the returns came pouring in. Most were the wrong size or wrong color and we just traded out. I only had to return money to one person. She had received a pair of boots and there was just no pleasing her! We were really happy to see the day end.

On my way home, Dean called to tell me they had Julie in custody and she would be here tomorrow. "Thank you, Dean. That was quick." "Well thanks to modern technology and the help of your daughter, it was a walk in the park."

Coming Home

Chapter 16

I am really reluctant about seeing her again. I know what she did was horrific but she is still my sister. She cost her husband and our parents their lives but at the same time she must be grieving too. At least I hope she is. It will be very hard to face her. I don't know what I will say. I am so hurt but am also feeling some compassion for her. I'm just so confused as how she could have been so cruel.

I took off at three and went to the San Marcos County Jail. I was sill having mixed feelings but Julie made it easy for me when I saw her. She was livid. She screamed at me. "Daddy fixed all my problems, then we covered it up and you had to come along and screw it all up! Oh yeah and nice job, burning the house down. Way to go Abby. Little Miss Abby. Always perfect, straight A's class president. I hated you when we got to college and I took the one thing you wanted most, Jimmy. He was a lousy husband, as you well know. I had it made when Daddy killed him but no, little Miss Abby had to fix that too. I was going to retire on the insurance money. All I had to do was wait seven years and I would be home free. Well the jokes on you Abby, cause I'm getting out of here and I can have the insurance money now. Get out of here. I don't want to see you. I never want to see you again. I hated you then and I hate you now."

I just stood in shock at the words. I held the tears until I was in the car. I immediately called Cade and asked if he could come over. He said "Now what's happened, Abby?" I told him and he said "I am in town. The hardware store burned to the ground and we are investigating it, I can be there in 10 minutes." "Could you make it around six? I am in San Marcos at the jail. I just visited with Julie." "Sure, Abby. I'll be there." I should have called Luke but he is just not good with things like this and I needed Cade's strong arms and compassion. I had not told Luke or Tessa Julie was here. I wanted to see her first.

Cade was at my door at six sharp. I didn't even worry about anyone seeing his truck. I just fell into his arms. He held on very tightly for a long time and I looked up at him and began to tell him the story of my

Coming Home

day. "She was a totally different person, Cade. I did not even reconize her. She told me she hated me. She hated me! After everything they had done, it was my fault it all fell apart." Cade just sat and listened as I paced back and forth. "She was horrible, telling me Daddy did her a favor by killing Jimmy. She didn't even bother to be concerned that our parents died. She was only interested in insurance money she will get." "I'm sorry Abby." "I was even feeling sorry for her on the way to the jail." We sat down on the couch and I said "I don't know what I would do without you." "Apparently you are my damsel in distress, and distress, and distress!" I laughed. "And you are my knight in shining armor."

"What is our relationship, Abby?" I was taken aback by his bluntness. "I don't really know, Cade." "You call me everytime you have a problem but as long as everything is fine, I hear nothing." "Oh, Cade, you are more than a friend could ever be. My feelings for you run deep." "But." "But I cannot hurt Luke. We have been through too much and he would be crushed if I left him. What about your girlfriend?" "It's a new relationship but I am very fond of her" "Fond of her?" "It's too early to tell. Damn it, Abby, I want you. Why do you think I come running everytime you call?" I was completely speechless. I was running things around in my head and none of it worked. "What should we do?" He stood up and ran his hand through his hair. "I want to be with you Cade, I just can't do it to Luke. He's been too good to me and Tessa. As much as I care for you, I just can't do it." "That pretty much says it all." He started for the door. "Cade, please wait." He stopped but did not turn around. I touched him on the shoulder and he turned. We looked in each others eyes and I said. "I need you in my life Cade, even if it means only now and then." "I feel the same but I don't know if I can keep my hands off of you for very long. I have only been seeing Terry for a short time but I enjoy her very much. She makes me laugh and seems to genuinely care about me. I've known who she was for years through friends but was married and never even thought about her in a loving way. Then we happen to be at a dance together and I kissed her, then left. A few phone calls and we started dating. That is how it all began and has progressed since then. I already feel a closeness to her that I want to explore but Abby, I still want you." I sat back down and said "What are we going to do?" He came, sat down beside me and took my hand. You once mentioned a vacation together every now and then." "Yes but now it sounds incredulous." "No it sounds exciting, passionate, and I think it would be an excellent way for us to be togther in our own way, forever." "It sounds so devious and almost cruel." "What is cruel about two people who care about each other as much as we do spending some private time together?" "What if we get caught? It's a small town and people talk. "The chances of that happeing are pretty slim. You see, that is what I was coming to talk to you about the day you found the letter. I got a job offer in Phoenix and I'm taking it. I move in three weeks." "Three weeks!" I felt a wave of panic come over me. I couldn't breathe but common sense finally hit me and I said. "I don't know what I will do without you but it sounds like that would be best for both of us."

I noticed car lights and my heart nearly jumped out of my chest. I waited for a knock on the door but Tessa just stormed in. She looked startled when she saw Cade standing there and he said "Ms Laurence if you need any other paper work about the fire, you just let me know." "Uh, thanks Mr. Tate. I appreciate you getting this to me so quickly." With a tip of his hat, he was gone. "Who was that? Wow, he's gorgeous." "Tessa, the man's old enough to be your father." "Oh well, it doesn't matter anyway. Dean called me today and told me Julie was in San Marcos. I came by to tell you she is dead to me. I went to see her and she said the most horrible cruel things to me." I held her and said "She did the same to me. Once her trial is over, I am done with her forever. I don't really care to ever lay eyes upon her again."

Chapter 17

Julie's trial started four months later. They brought her into the courtroom in an orange jumpsuit and handcuffs. Her hair was a little longer and in dire need of some attention. She looked awful, and when she looked at me I felt shivers run down my spine. How could someone I loved so much turn out to be, for lack of a better word, a demon? She hid her emotions well when we were young. Maybe I was just too into myself that I didn't notice. I thought we had the perfect sister relationship back then. Jimmy could not have caused all this, it had to be underlying for years. That much hatred for someone you spent everyday with had to mess with your head.

Coming Home

The judge called the room to order and the District Attorney began with his opening speech to the jury, followed by her attorney. She had him flown in from New York. Even though Jimmy left his life insurance to Tessa, Julie was very well off, and could afford the best. He is a pompous ass, and has the attitude that we are a bunch of country bumpkins. That did not set well with the judge when they had her bail hearing.

She could have plead guilty and this would all be over but she thinks her lawyer will get her off, so opted for a jury trial. Despite the attorney's best efforts, the judge considered Julie a flight risk so would not set bail. She has been in the Hays County jail all this time.

The defense called their first witness to the stand. Ms. Abigail Laurence. I am so nervous but make my way to the stand. "Place your right hand on the Bible. Do you solemnly swear to tell the truth, the whole truth, and nothing but the truth, so help you God?" "I do." "You may sit down and state your full name." "Abigail Laurence."

Mr. Pompous Ass stood and walk toward me and asked "Ms. Laurence, what is your relationship to the defendant?" "She is my twin sister." He looks at the jury and then turns back to me. "Is it true, Ms. Laurence, that your twin sister, the defendant, stole your husband and father of your child, and in fact was having an affair with him the whole time you were married?" "I recently found that to be true, yes."

Darla Hagan

"How did that make you feel?" "Objection, relevance?" "I am trying to establish the relationship between the defendant and Ms. Laurence, You Honor." "Over ruled, continue." "How did that make you feel, Ms. Laurence." "I was shocked." "Shocked? Shocked enough to concoct this crazy story about your parents killing" "Objection, badgering the witness." "Sustained. Watch yourself counselor." "Ms. Laurence, were you jealous of your sister? She had your husband, his wealth, and his love." "I did not know any of this until after the fact." "You are telling me and this jury that all these years, you never suspected your husband was with your sister?" "No, I had no reason to think that. My sister would not have anything to do with Jimmy. When we got married she would not even come around. After our divorce the only contact I had with him was through the court. Julie had left long before that." "Objection, Judge, what is the defense looking for?" "Get to the point counselor." "Your Honor, I am trying to show the members of the jury that Ms. Laurence is a scorned wife out for revenge." "Objection, Your Honor." "Sustained. Counselor, move on." "No more questions, Your Honor."

"Your witness." "Thank you, Your Honor." "Ms. Laurence, when did you learn of your husbands infidelity." "Right after Christmas, when I read a letter that my parents had left for me." "Where did you find this letter?" "After my house burned, they were removing the bricks of the fireplace, and came across a box behind one of the bricks. The letter was in the box." "What else was in the box, Ms. Laurence?" "It was a time capsule that we as a family did many years ago. Julie and I were suppose to open it on our fiftieth birthday." "You opened it before that. Why?" "Given the loss of my parents, I thought it might be good to remember the good times with my daughter." "Your Honor, I place into evidence exhibit A, the letter of which Ms. Laurence speaks." "So be it." "Ms. Laurence, would you read the letter to the jury?" I was shaking when he handed it to me but proceeded through tears to read my parents final words. "Your Honor, the prosecution rests."

Final arguments were made by both attorneys and Julie's was still trying to make me out to be the bad guy. Court was adjourned while the jury deliberated. We walked out of the courthouse to get some fresh air, and the District attorney said it would be short and sweet. "There is no way that jury could not see what was done." "I hope you are right, I want this to be over, so we can all move on with our lives." "Would you like to go get a cup of coffee while we wait?" "That would be great." Tessa and I walked across the street with him and sat at a small cafe to wait.

We had just finished our coffee when he got a call saying the jury was back with a verdict. "So soon! Is that good?" "Let's just go and take our seats." When the Judge came back in the room, the bailiff bellowed "All rise." When the Judge sat down, the bailiff again bellowed "Be seated." The Judge looked up to see if everyone was in place and proceeded to ask the jury if they had reached a verdict. "We have your honor." "Would you please give the verdict to the bailiff?" The foreman handed the paper to the bailiff who in turn gave it to the Judge. "Will the defendant please rise to receive your verdict?" Julie and her attorney rose and awaited the news. The judge read "We the jury, find the defendant Julie Laurence, guilty of the charges of conspiracy." Julie looked at her attorney and then looked at me with that bone chilling stare. The judge sentenced her to five years in a minimum security facility with a chance for parole in two years. She started screaming at me "This isn't over bitch. You will not ruin my life again." They took her out and Tessa and I hugged each other with tears.

The weeks turned into months and Luke continues to come every other weekend. Julie is in a small town not far from San Marcos. I am sure with her personality the way it is she will be the perfect angel and get out in two years. I pray she finds regret and doesn't live with this hatred anymore. Tessa put the insurance money from Jimmy to work for her and decided to get her Masters Degree. It is the one decent thing Jimmy did in his life.

As for me. I continue to enjoy myself running my little shop and spending time with Luke in my lovely new home. As for Cade, Terri got transferred to Albuquerque so they are doing the long distance thing also. We text often and are still looking for a time to be together but have not as yet...

Coming Home

Darla Hagan

About the Author

I am the mother of two beautiful daughters, three adorable granddaugthers, one handsome grandson, and the most precious great-granddaughter ever. I started writing when I lost my husband of thirty-three years to cancer. The writing seems to take up a lot of lonely hours. I live in Texas with my two cats Ollie and Delilah and spend time in Virginia every year. I have two wonderful sisters and two very special brothers in-law. My mother is ninety two and has more energy than all of us put together. I love the outdoors and the beach is one of my favorite places to write. There is just something about the sound of the sea that frees your mind. I have come to love writing and look forward to publishing many more books.

www.ingramcontent.com/pod-product-compliance
Lightning Source LLC
Chambersburg PA
CBHW071458040426
42444CB00008B/1398